Compass

To —

Tom and Kathy —

My brother and sister
in Christ who persever with me
to become people who reflect God's
character and intentionally guide
children's spiritual and character
formation toward God.

I praise God for your
faithful friendship, prayers and
unconditional love!

Venice

Luke 18:16

2-12-09

Cover: Kathryn Baker Schorr

Printed in the United States of America

For permission to use material, contact:
Vernie Schorr
Character Choice
1545 Tanaka Drive
Erie, Colorado 80516
303.828.3648
vschorr@characterchoice.org

ISBN: 1-4392-1247-3
EAN13: 9781439212479
LCCN: 2008908822

Visit www.booksurge.com to order additional copies.

C&mpass

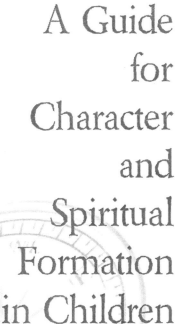

A Guide
for
Character
and
Spiritual
Formation
in Children

VERNIE SCHORR

To my grandchildren Geoff, Sarah, Stefanie, Hannah, and Thomas. You are my joy. Watching each of you continue to make choices that form your character and spirit in Christlikeness tells me there is great hope and adventure for your generation.

To advocates of children. Never, never, never, give up.

Contents

Acknowledgments

THIS BOOK, as most books, is an adventure and product of many people.

I am so grateful for my team of facilitators who have spent hours brainstorming how to make the forming of character and conscience concrete for children. Thank you for your multiple hours of travel, training, and practice with me throughout the world, discovering together the joy of guiding children to know and love God and be formed by His character.

My thanks to the parents and teachers who have shared their stories and teaching experiences with me.

I especially want to thank my board members Sharon Floyd, Tom Forbes, Sterling Lands II, and Kathy and Tom Palmer for their encouragement and support in this project.

Kudos to others who over many years continued to persuade me to write this book, especially Carolyn Depolo, Barbara Frick, Carol Long, Linda Mahley, and Marilyn Shaver.

The people in my small groups, you know who you are. Your prayers, concern, encouragement, and accountability required me to never, never, never give up.

I am deeply grateful for the patient and constructive editing and help of Karen Roberts. The book would not have been completed without her.

Thanks to my reviewers Lorie Barnes, Barbara Bingham, Kathleen Chapman, Chap Clark, Judy Comstock, Tom Forbes, Deb Hansen, Tracy Mancino, Ruth McKee, Tom Palmer, and Libby Vincent.

Most of all, I am grateful to God that His character is immeasurably full of grace, compassion, forgiveness, and integrity and never changes.

Introduction

"Do not be misled: bad company corrupts good character."
1 Corinthians 15:33

So, you are interested in character formation! That's why you are looking at this book and preparing to purchase it, or someone thinks you need to be interested in it because that person has sent this book to you as a gift.

I am passionate about character and spiritual formation. My vision is to see children, youth, and adults reflecting God's character, leading godly lives, and practicing biblically based life skills that impact and transform broken societies worldwide. I have spent the last twenty-two years pursuing this vision and seeing it become a reality through training and equipping those who serve children.

The goal of this book is to equip you, the reader, with greater understanding of character and spiritual formation and with proven methods, materials, and tools to pursue this vision too. Together we can become part of the solution, instilling roots of positive character, conscience, and conduct in the lives of children, youth, and other adults.

I have a question for you. Where are you in your personal character and spiritual formation and your effectiveness in guiding the character and spiritual formation of the children God has placed in your life?

In the late 1980s, I was challenged to begin thinking about and writing materials for what was being called at that time "character education curriculum." As I explored the many facets of character and conscience and their formation within individuals, something totally unexpected happened. I was confronted by my own poverty of character.

The realization that in all my education and serving in areas of Christian education I had learned next to nothing concrete about character virtues or the formation of character hit me hard. Oh, I knew right from wrong. Most of the time, I was kind and considerate. I was fortunate enough to have been raised when our culture intrinsically exampled a flavor of compassion, integrity, respect, and responsibility. I believed in God, Jesus, and the Holy Spirit. I had accepted Christ as my personal Savior and Lord. And I knew the call on my life: to guide children to come to know Jesus, choose to believe God's promises, and learn to live the abundant life with the help and guidance of the Holy Spirit.

As I wrote training and curriculum materials about compassion, I had to face my own compassion attitudes. When traveling, I caught myself being indifferent about my fellow travelers. Writing about integrity was a huge hurdle too. Raised in an alcoholic home, I had learned to lie as a way of survival. As an adult, this habit turned into acceptable and at times attractive exaggeration.

I could go on, but what I want to communicate is twofold. First, the freedom to respond to life and people with beliefs and attitudes that heal, instill love and forgiveness, and bring personal joy and peace comes from life with God in a lifelong process of becoming a person who reflects God's character. Second is the importance of showing the world your desire and perseverance to become a reflection of God's character, driven by an orderly process of spiritual formation in Christ.

Becoming a person who reflects God's character requires understanding and believing what is true to the real world. What I mean by the term "real world" is, in Eugene Peterson's words, "the God-created, God-saved, God-blessed, God-ruled world in which we find ourselves."[1] Becoming people who reflect God's character is about developing virtues, good habits, attitudes, dispositions, and spiritual disciplines that lead children to responsible and mature adulthood. Character and spiritual formation begins in children as they respond to the character and spiritual formation reflected by those adults who are their parents, teachers, or coaches. To say it another way, the character of the adults who influence a child is a primary factor in the forming of positive (God's) or negative character in that child's life.

Regardless of where you are in your own character and spiritual formation at this moment, it is important for you to attempt to understand and believe what is true to the real world in which we live. The ideas and beliefs you hold have defined consequences.

How do you know the beliefs you hold are true?

Why do you NOT go and jump off a roof, a cliff, or some other high place? If you did, why would you fall to the ground? If your answer is "because of gravity," then I know that you know something that is true about the real world in which we live. You can't see gravity or hold it in your hands, but it describes something that is true about the world. As a result of what you believe about gravity, you behave accordingly. In other words, your understanding of reality affects how you behave.

What if you decided that you no longer believed in the law of gravity? Sooner or later you would act on that belief and step off a roof or cliff. You might even enjoy the ride down, until the crushing realization hit you that your belief was wrong.

Just as you understand and believe in gravity, it is important for you to understand and believe what is true to the real world in relationship to the forming of character and spirit that is taking place in the lives of children in today's culture. The tragic high school, university, and mall shootings are real evidence. Children and youth in this country are being raised without a sense of belonging or a firm moral foundation. They act and react without a clear understanding of right and wrong and the consequences of their behaviors.

The first two stories you are about to read in Chapter One are shocking and disturbing. They are two of many real-life stories that compel us to take a closer look at character and spiritual formation at the earliest ages. Each chapter that follows offers additional, real-life stories and examples to help drive home the point of the chapter. At the end of each chapter, you have opportunities to reflect on and also to practice what you have just read.

I am excited that you want to do more to guide the formation of God's character in the children entrusted to your care. You are joining me on a journey that will transform your life as well as the lives of your children.

NOTES

[1] Eugene H. Peterson, *The Jesus Way: A Conversation on the Ways That Jesus Is the Way* (Grand Rapids, Mich.: William B. Eerdmans, 2007), 1.

CHAPTER ONE

The Why and What of Character Formation

"Do not be conformed to this world, but be transformed by the
renewing of your minds, so that you may discern what is the will
of God—what is good and acceptable and perfect."
Romans 12:2 (NRSV)

A young man leaned over the crib of his firstborn son. He opened a blue velvet box, removed the tiny silver necklace, and placed it around the neck of his baby. Gently touching the silver initials GLB, the father whispered to his son, "This necklace marks you as a Gang Land Baby. I will teach you how to get anything you want. No one will ever cross you without the consequence of experiencing a violent or deadly response. At the moment of your birth, you became a member of the gang. You will always belong to the gang and live by our code!"

This young man had attended a middle school and high school in a suburban U.S. community. Gang activity in these schools had motivated the school board and administration to establish a strong set of standards and discipline. Even though this young man continued his membership in the local gang, he remained in school. The staff encouraged and mentored him in hopes of building his character and conscience toward good.

Three months before his high school graduation, the local gang leader was killed. The gang chose this young man to become the new leader. No amount of persuasion, care, or concern from others could change his mind. He left school without graduating.

This young man now lives in a palatial home on a hill with his "lady," drives a large black limousine, and has vowed to raise his child according to beliefs, attitudes, actions, and the gang codes of self-indulgence, indifference, violence, dishonesty, and revenge.

Following is another true story, this one told to me by Margaret Bridges, a colleague of mine.

While in Romania we visited an orphanage. As we entered, we became aware of only one light bulb, so we couldn't see, but the smell was awful. The question came to mind, were chickens being kept in here? There was the sound of a dripping tap.

Next we could see that there was wire up and around little wire beds, and in those beds were little babies. They were not crying. They didn't cry, we understood later, because they had already learned that their cries would not bring anyone to their little wired boxes. These babies had never experienced the wonderful feeling and attachment a little child has by having its needs meet.

The babies in this orphanage were under-indulged, never touched, and never bonded. They would grow to adulthood in the orphanage, still un-bonded, under-indulged, and with the knowledge that they had been abandoned. Because bonding never took place, trust was absent, abandonment beliefs and attitudes were engrained, and character and conscience were not formed toward good.

Nicolae Ceausescu, who led Romania as a neo-Stalinist police state from 1967–1989, was able to choose these boys to torture people because they never felt like they were persons of value. Their conscience was seared and character malformed.

Extreme, you say? Maybe, but these two stories show the tragic results that can happen when children grow into adulthood without the love, nurture, and guidance of adults whose lives reflect character and conscience shaped toward good (God).

Children entrusted to us are in similar situations. Some are overindulged, some un-bonded, and some have the sense of being unattached and abandoned. Think of the children you know who seem unattached except to their stuff or their peers. They struggle with what it means to trust someone. Right and wrong are rationalized.

Chap Clark, president of Foothill Community Ministries and associate professor of youth, family and culture at Fuller Theological Seminary, has complied some disturbing research that reveals the present attitude of much of our society toward our young. In his book entitled *Hurt*, he writes: "I come to believe that we as a society have allowed institutions and systems originally designed to nurture children and adolescents to lose their missional mandate. In other words, society has systemically abandoned the young."[1]

The Case for Positive Character Formation

Here is another story, one that offers hope.

"Nicolas without an 'h'" is how a shy four-year-old answered me when I greeted him by saying, "Good morning, my name is Ms. Vernie. Please tell me your name." Nicolas had noticed, when looking at his name tag, that I had spelled his name NICHOLAS. Nicolas's shyness was the least of his challenges. He readily communicated that he needed a great deal of help to accomplish a simple task.

Those of us involved in intentionally developing the virtue of responsibility in Nicolas's class had been encouraging and requiring Nicolas to become a responsible person. Continued reinforcements of the attitudes and actions of responsible people were described. We used character language, practice, and praise. "People of responsibility gather their cup and napkin and place them in the trash basket when they are finished with their snack. Thank you, Nicolas." "You are a responsible person when you return the markers to the basket before leaving the table."

One morning Nicolas's classmate, four-year-old Celie, remarked to the class, "Have you noticed that Nicolas finds his place on the circle without being reminded? He is becoming a responsible person." Some weeks later, Nicolas was heard commenting to his father, "Dad, I am a responsible person. I can find my coat and put it on without help."

What makes the difference in this story compared to the two earlier ones?

In the first, the young man had been exposed early and often to violence, revenge, and greed through the gang code and activities in his community. Efforts by parents and significant people at school during the young man's teen years had not been enough to counteract the culture and resulting destructive character formation.

In the second, the children in the orphanage were denied the bonding, example, formation of trust, and instruction concerning right and wrong that are required for the development and formation of character and conscience toward good. Their lives reflected their poverty of character and conscience.

In the third, Nicolas internalized responsibility at a very young age through the labeling, practice, and praise he received from his teachers, peers, and family. The inward transformation became apparent and natural in his outward attitudes and actions.

The business, education, and faith communities of the United States share a growing consensus that over the past two decades, our cultures have experienced a steep decline in civility, morality, and harmony. This decline is confirmed by the communal plea for more books, programs, seminars, training, and educational materials that address character and conscience development, moral values, and servant leadership.

There is a general recognition that our nation's cultures at present are often more successful at developing people to be self-indulgent than at nurturing them in the pursuit of altruistic, servant leadership virtues. Commercial television, film, and music industries convey the belief that the measure of success in society is the accumulation of material wealth and the frequency of experiences of sensual pleasure and adrenaline rushes. This stridently secular humanistic definition of success stands in sharp contrast to biblical principles and beliefs. To the point of this book, it stands contrary to the character, conscience, and spirit we need to be developing in our children.

Biblical principles and beliefs articulate the positive outcomes of moderate pursuit of sensual experiences. They indicate that the battlefield is the minds of our children, which are being filled today with post-modern philosophies and worldviews that give little ground to timeless biblical truths. The battle itself is spiritual. Our goal must be to impact the will, engage the minds, and develop the character, conscience, and spirit of children in such a manner that they form beliefs that drive behavior, attitudes and language that drive actions, and character that drives conduct, each one reflecting the character of God and transformed values.

Character, Character Education, and Character Formation

The idea of character education has captured the attention of the White House and Congress, both of which are searching for the appropriate federal role in promoting basic decency. Lawmakers have lent their symbolic support by endorsing "National Character Counts Week." The Department of Education has funded a few character pilot programs. Many states have also created character education requirements.

To understand character education, we must first understand what character is and how it is formed. We can then begin to understand the larger concept of character and spiritual formation, which goes far beyond character education.

The word *character* is used in a variety of ways. It is sometimes used to describe a person in a book or play. Sometimes it is used to describe a personality, as in "She's a character," implying a positive or negative attribute of the person. These and other uses of the word *character* may create confusion about its use in this book. For the purposes of this book, when I speak of character, I am speaking of a person's inward nature. Its appearance may be constructive or destructive.

Author Dallas Willard defines character in this way: "Our character is that internal, overall structure of the self that is revealed by our long-run patterns of behavior and from which our actions more or less automatically arise."[2]

Character is formed both intentionally and unintentionally. The intentional positive character formation that once was an intrinsic part of our culture has been replaced with the model of serving self and seeking fame, sexual promiscuity, violence, blame, revenge, and a host of other destructive traits. The result is unintentional formation of these destructive character traits. The outcomes of both the intentional and the unintentional define a person's approach to life and worldview.

The good news is that character can be changed. That is what godly character and spiritual formation is about.

Dallas Willard says, "The Spirit of God now calls his people to live from an adequate basis for character transformation, resulting in obedience to and abundance in Christ."[3] Our task, as advocates of children, is twofold: to become intentional in our own personal character and spiritual formation toward God and, in turn, to become intentional in our children's character and spiritual formation. In doing so, we reflect God's character and build a conscience that chooses right from wrong.

Thankfully, God's character, revealed to us in the life of Christ, offers hope for character and spiritual transformation even in the worst of circumstances. There is hope! It is possible, and it is an adventure.

The Adventure Ahead

As a follower of Christ, I work with educators and parents around the country to bring an awareness of the need to change the poverty of character and searing of conscience in our children. I have seen the benefits of intentionally developing character and conscience in children. I have also witnessed character and spiritual transformation in the lives of children whose early character and spiritual formation was less than ideal.

At the early ages (children age 2–11), the focus of character development is on the *prevention* of moral decay. At the middle and upper ages (youth age 12–18), the focus shifts to *intervention* in the midst of moral decay. This book's emphasis is what we can do to help in the forming of character at the early ages to prevent moral decay.

At the middle and upper ages (youth age 12–18), the focus shifts to intervention in the midst of moral decay.

Forming character is more than learning about or changing behavior. Character formation requires the intentional training and developing of spirit, will, and mind toward God. It involves truth seeking and the discovering of beliefs that transform the spirit. It requires a commitment of the adults in our society to reinvest in the lives of individual young people. Our nation's culture itself is no longer as attentive to the needs of children as it once was. Our task, therefore, is to be intentional about meeting the need for character development and formation in children.

I am writing with a deep passion and belief, based on years of ministry with children and educators of children, that character is formed in every child either toward good (God) or evil. My challenge is to make you, the reader, aware of the importance of your task, as a children's advocate, to become intentional about developing God's character in yourself and in the children you influence.

In this book you are introduced to eight foundation virtues based on God's character, family virtues that form from the foundation virtues, and virtue definitions. You are given a process for the forming of character, a proven learning cycle to enable inward transformation, character language using guided conversation skills, questions through which you may build and filter a learner's biblical worldview, and age level strategies to develop spiritual disciplines. At the end of each chapter, you have the opportunity to apply what you learn to yourself and to your learners.

Are you ready for the adventure?

NOTES

[1] Chap Clark, *Hurt* (Grand Rapids, MI: Baker Academic, 2004), 36.
[2] Dallas Willard, *Renovation of the Heart* (Colorado Springs, CO: NavPress, 2002), 142.
[3] Ibid., 25.

Think on These Things

Character and spiritual formation is taking place daily in you and your learners. Who and what is forming your character and spirit?

_____

_____

_____

Who and what is forming your learners' character and spirit?

_____

_____

_____

(Hint: This is not deep theology. Think in terms of everyday mainte-nance, events, time spent, heroes, media, and fads. Be specific.)

Practice It!

Take some time right now to identify some of the personal qualities, beliefs, virtues, principles, and values that you presently hold. (You may choose to invite a friend to do this exercise with you.) Please follow these four steps:

1. Locate an 8½" x 11" piece of blank paper, and fold it twice to form eight rectangular boxes. When I do this exercise with children, I give them a choice of folding the piece of paper in a "hot dog" fold (folding the paper in half lengthwise) or a "hamburger" fold (folding the paper in half width-wise). Integrating the opportunity to make choices is a crucial intervention in character development. So have a little fun making your choice.

2. In each box, write a personal quality/idea/principle/belief you want to develop or continue to develop for yourself. Hint: Think about something you wish to pass on to others. Some ideas to stimulate your thinking are:

> compassion
>
> respect
>
> handling money wisely
>
> enjoying music
>
> having meaningful relationships
>
> having a personal relationship with Jesus

3. Next, tear your paper along the fold lines into eight rectangles, and place the eight pieces in the order of importance to you—number 1 being the most important.

4. If possible, share with another person what you decided to be number 1 and number 2, telling why you chose them.

Have you finished? Congratulations. By putting these personal qualities/ideas/principles/beliefs in the order of importance to you and then sharing your reasons for your choices, you have indicated some of the ideology, philosophy, theology, beliefs, character virtues, and values you hold to be true.

I hope that this exercise has helped you to begin to think about character formation and your individual set of beliefs. As advocates of children, we have the awesome responsibility to be examples of God's character. I am pleased that you want to be a person who reflects God's character. I am excited that you want to do more to develop God's character in your life and the lives of the children entrusted to your care.

CHAPTER TWO

Begin at the Beginning

"God is working in you to help you want to do what pleases him.
Then he gives you the power to do it."
Philippians 2:13 (ICB)

O ur character is made up of those ideas, principles, and personal qualities that give life direction, meaning, and depth. Character constitutes our inner sense of what is right and wrong based on who we are, not on external laws or rules of conduct. It is our character that drives our conduct, and it is our character that forms our attitudes, choices, and actions, which demonstrate who we are and who we are becoming.

Our choice to become people who reflect God's character becomes evident as we live in and live out character virtues such as compassion, forgiveness, and integrity. The living in and living out of these virtues, in the likeness of Christ, is the evidence of our inner transformation. That inner transformation happens as a result of both our conscious effort and the work of the Spirit of God.

Character Formation

The forming of character is a lifelong process. Character develops and forms through thoughts, words, attitudes, actions, relationships, choices, and conflict. Character formation begins in infancy, both intentionally and without intention, and extends throughout life.

Everyone receives some type of character formation, just as everyone receives some type of education. The question is, what is the standard and model for the character being developed? Is the standard and model character traits such as indifference, revenge, or subtle dishonesty (e.g., it is okay to tell a white lie)? Or is the standard based on God's character as revealed in God's book the Bible and modeled by Christ's life and words?

I am passionate about *godly character formation,* which is the intentional training of spirit and mind toward Christ. It includes identified *dos* and *don'ts* of life with others. It involves relationships, rules, and precepts. It is wrong to steal from others, abuse children, kill another person, or lie to parents or friends. It is right to return a lost article to its owner, to tell the truth, to help a neighbor, and forgive a wrong.

> *Godly character formation is the intentional training of spirit and mind toward Christ.*

Godly character formation requires the intentional and personal involvement of others in the process with example, instruction, and training (practice) in good habits that affect a person's pattern of behavior, personality, and moral strength. Practical examples of intentional involvement, example, instruction, and practice are found throughout this book.

Godly character formation also requires each person to assume responsibility within one's self for thoughts, words, and actions. And it requires people to live out their own inward transformation. Perhaps most important of all, godly character formation enables the transfer of beliefs, attitudes, and character virtues to others, launching benefit to families, communities, and societies.

The intentional developing of character in the children we serve is more than simply directing them to behave in certain ways. It is more than posting a character virtue word on a bulletin board. It includes equipping children to think, to discern, to ask questions, and to evaluate answers. It requires creating opportunities for children to actively participate in making choices and decisions and to experience the consequences of their choices and decisions. And it requires practice and habit forming. Together these tasks and activities result in character formation in the likeness of Christ and internal character transformation that result in the outward living of God's character.

Character Transformation

Character formation is outward, so I speak of the teaching, developing, and forming of character as outward formation. *Character transformation*, on the other hand, is what takes place inwardly. We know that inward transformation is taking place when the character being formed outwardly is lived out when no one is instructing, correcting, or requiring character conduct, attitudes, or belief. Inward transformation is the transformation of the spirit (will) and conscience.

> Character formation is outward.

Dallas Willard's words capture our task well. "Character formation is not behavior modification."[1] It is much more. In fact, character formation and spiritual formation are inseparable. Character formation impacts spiritual formation. Spiritual formation impacts character formation. The two interact and impact each other.

> *Character transformation* is what takes place inwardly.

Willard clarifies the difference for us between spiritual formation and Christian spiritual formation. "Spiritual formation, without regard to any specifically religious context or tradition, is the process by which the human spirit or will is given a definite form, or character."[2] He goes on to say, "Christian spiritual formation, in contrast, is the redemptive process of forming the inner human world so that it takes on the character of the inner being of Christ himself."[3]

Character and spiritual transformation are taking place within every human being throughout life. The earlier a child is exposed to constructive character formation, the earlier virtue habits transform the mind, will, and conscience into Christlikeness. At the earliest possible age, therefore, a child may be guided to become aware of life with God. A phrase I like to use with children is that we have a "with-God life." He helps us to be people who show God's character to others.

Be aware that inward transformation becomes either constructive or destructive, and it is the compelling reason for intentionally developing character and conscience toward God. Constructive character formation and transformation happen more fully when children know how deeply they are loved by parents, grandparents, teachers, and other significant adults. Parents and family members are the primary teachers of their children. Henrietta Mears, founder of Gospel Light Publications, often said, "First a child learns to love their 'teacher' and then their teacher's God." In other words, character is more effectively formed and trans-formed when children first know that they are the loved by teachers, parents, or significant adults, and then they can come to know that they are loved by God.

In recent years there has been an emphasis on building a child's self-esteem. This emphasis has not been as successful as some had hoped. I believe the reason is that building self without the transformation of self by God's character sets up a child to be ruled by the "kingdom" of self rather than the "kingdom" of God.

The indispensable foundation of character transformation is the replacement of the natural (old self) with the formation of God's character in us (new self). This transformation is accomplished as we surrender to the Spirit of God to transform His character in us.

Character transformation is not an automatic response. It requires our effort through individual choices, beliefs, attitudes, language, and actions to cooperate with the work of God's Spirit. The process is described in God's book the Bible. "God working in your to help you want to do what pleases him. Then he gives you the power to do it" (Philippians 2:13, ICB).

God's transforming work gives us hope that the destructive character unintentionally or intentionally developed and formed early in children is not set in stone. It is another compelling reason to be deliberate and intentional at the earliest age about developing beliefs, attitudes, and character habits in children that result in their inner transformation to become people who reflect God's character.

A Proven Learning Process

Those who teach and serve with me believe that learning is a process that follows an effectively used pattern. Building character and conscience requires such a process. We have discovered that inward character transformation occurs more readily though an intentionally defined and proven learning process.

This proven learning process enables a trusted adult to guide learners into an inward transformation that enables them to transfer, or pass on, their character virtues to others. Understanding this learning process allows parents and educators to plan a variety of experiences that build character and conscience.

Learners, both children and adults, process information in different ways. The best learning takes place when the children are actively involved. Some children require many tactile, hands-on experiences. Others require various kinesthetic, movement activities. Others may need auditory, spoken instructions or visual stimuli such as pictures and graphics to assimilate information. Most learners require a combination of one or more of these ways.

Here is a description of the process I have used successfully to introduce character virtues to children. Note that it begins with providing ways to help children focus and become ready to be engaged. The process assumes a somewhat structured classroom or home school experience, but it also may be experienced in part or whole in unplanned, teachable moments.

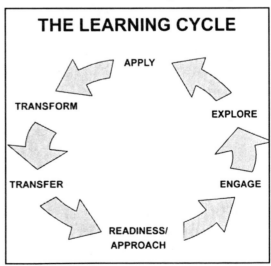

THE LEARNING CYCLE

APPLY

TRANSFORM

EXPLORE

TRANSFER

ENGAGE

READINESS/
APPROACH

READINESS/APPROACH

Readiness/approach activities begin when the first learner arrives (when the learning experience where you are being intentional about a character virtue begins). The purpose of these activities is to create a readiness for learning or to reinforce previous concepts. For example, a leader or parent can use a puppet to give the definition of a character virtue or to give a listening assignment before a story. "Listen and be ready to tell who was responsible in this story." Readiness activities at the beginning of a session motivate learners to develop an attitude that says, "I want to learn."

Readiness/approach activities may serve other purposes as well. They often enable learners to remember an idea or to understand relationships between ideas. They also can provide a foundation on which to build the session story and character concepts that follow. Finally, readiness activities create a link between multiple sessions so learners can better understand the logical sequence of concepts.

ENGAGE

Engage is the next part of the learning process. Here character virtues and biblical principles are presented through storytelling and example. The leader reads or tells a story that is centered on a specific piece of literature, historical character, event, or Bible passage that communicates or illustrates the central idea of the virtue being taught. Providing a series of questions to provoke discussion of the story helps children think critically, remember, and begin to apply ideas from the story to their lives.

EXPLORE

After engaging learners, the leader provides experiences for children to explore the concepts they are being led to learn. The learners are not mere spectators or listeners but central and active

participants in the learning process. Children are more likely to enjoy learning when they can make choices and are successful in the tasks they accomplish.

Character virtue activities at this stage of the process are designed to involve children in the continued exploration of truth. These activities allow the use of all five senses, the opportunity to make more choices, and to make life applications. Activities are varied to include art, music, drama, oral and written communication, science, puzzles, and games.

APPLY

The learning process now motivates learners to begin to apply or put discovered truth into practice, with a peer or others, within safe relationships. For example, practice takes place as children participate in a drama about requiring acts of forgiveness. It is important to note that this stage requires supervised practice where the leader, educator, or parent encourages, reminds, and identifies the application of the target virtue.

TRANSFORMATION

As the learners apply the virtue being formed, the inward transformation begins. Learners assume responsibility for the virtue within themselves, and they demonstrate living out their private, inward transformation in situations inside and outside of the learning environment. The character virtue learned actually changes and molds their thinking, words, attitudes, actions, and conscience. It is at this stage that children begin to perceive the necessity of being a person who reflects God's character. For example, a child may choose to play with the new neighbor or student even though his friends want him to play only with them.

TRANSFER

After transformation, the learning process enables learners to pass on, or transfer, the character virtue forming in them to others: families, friends, communities, and societies. An example is the child who chooses to play with the new neighbor or student instead of his friends. The friends see his choice and action, and they are influenced by it to play with the new person also.

Although the illustration of the learning process is depicted as a cycle, the learning is an ongoing process. It is, however, neither automatic nor linear. Children may progress through the cycle at different rates and may need to return for reinforcement at any point in the process.

NOTES

[1] Dallas Willard, *Renovation of the Heart* (Colorado Springs, CO: NavPress, 2002), 25.

[2] Dallas Willard, *The Great Omission* (San Francisco: Harper, 2006), 104.

[3] Ibid., 105.

Think on These Things

Try putting into your own words the meaning of "character formation."

_____

_____

_____

Practice It!

"Compassion is sympathy for someone else's suffering or misfortune, together with the desire to help, and appropriate action for his or her benefit."

Create a readiness activity to introduce this definition of compassion. Hint: First identify the age of the child(ren), and then think of a concrete way to demonstrate or illustrate helping, caring, or sharing.

_____

_____

_____

_____

How are you doing? Do you need more help with your readiness activity? Look at the readiness activities in the sample sessions in the Appendix for some other ideas.

CHAPTER THREE

Three Principles of Character Formation

"Therefore as God's chosen people, holy and dearly loved, clothe yourselves with compassion, kindness, humility, gentleness and patience. Bear with each other and forgive whatever grievances you may have against one another. Forgive as the Lord forgave you. And over all these virtues put on love."

Colossians 3:12–14a

Becoming people who live out and reflect God's character doesn't just happen. The challenge is to lay a solid foundation for character development and formation at the earliest age. There are three fundamental principles to understand and put into practice as you guide the character and spiritual formation of children.

Principle 1: Beliefs Drive Behavior

Dallas Willard describes belief as "when your whole being is set to act as if something is so."[1] Beliefs have consequences. Beliefs drive behavior.

> Beliefs drive behavior.
> Attitudes drive actions.
> Character drives conduct.

What beliefs do you hold? How do you know they are true? What is your standard for truth?

Remember the exercise you did at the end of Chapter One to identify some of the personal qualities, beliefs, virtues, principles, and values that you presently hold? If you are able, find the rectangle in that exercise that you identified as number one. What would be some implications of holding and living out the quality that you believe in strongly enough to have put it as first place? Take a moment to note some implications.

For example, if my number one choice were enjoying music, some consequences might be sacrifices of time and money, patience while listening to beginner's practicing and playing in recitals, as well as the need to examine the message of the music I enjoy.

Now ask yourself this question. What do the children you influence believe?

Robert Coles, in his book *The Spiritual Life of Children*,[2] relates that the questions "'Where Do We Come From? What Are We? And Where Are We Going?' are the eternal questions children ask more intensely, unremittingly, and subtly than we sometimes imagine." It seems reasonable, therefore, to create biblical answers to these questions as well as others to help your children develop a consistent set of beliefs (biblical worldview).

I believe that it is an important exercise to create a simple set of questions to help develop a useful and consistent set of beliefs through which the chil-

> Create a simple set of questions to help develop a useful and consistent set of beliefs.

dren you serve may be helped to understand the myriad of thoughts, words, attitudes, and actions that bombard them daily. The questions that you create must truly operate on the basis of God's principles, His expectations, and sound reasoning from Scripture. Articulating the answers to these questions clearly for your children is imperative. They must also be repeated throughout all of the spiritual and character development experiences you create for your children.

The purpose of these questions is to help the leader, teacher, and parent guide children to develop a biblical worldview of life and help them discover how to live it out consistently in their everyday life. Since the questions are for use with children, remember to keep them simple, concrete, and practical for their use in understanding God's truth and principles. Here is a set of questions I created.

Practical Questions to Facilitate a Comprehensive Understanding of God's Character, Truth, and Principles (Biblical Worldview)

Who made God?

What is the character and nature of God?

Why did God create the world and all that is within it?

How did God create all things?

Why did God make people?

What does God care about?

Who is Jesus?

Who is the Holy Spirit?

What is truth?

What am I thankful for?

Is there really a being named Satan?

What happens after our bodies die on earth?

"But how do I use the questions?" you ask. Good question. Creating them is first and foremost an exercise for you. It forces you to focus on your basic beliefs. You must then articulate biblically based answers for the questions that your children can understand. For example, you might ask yourself, what do I know and believe to be true about the

Holy Spirit? What Bible content or verses confirm these truths? To formulate your answer, you would need to ask what terms, language, examples, and activities are age-level appropriate to teach these truths to your children. You would then devise your answer carefully. Please do not succumb to the erroneous thinking that children are too young to learn these truths.

An example of how you might answer the question about the Holy Spirit could be: "The Holy Spirit is our helper and guide. He gives power to choose what is right (John 14). He gives love. He gives joy. He gives peace. He gives patience, kindness, goodness, faithfulness, and gentleness. And He even gives self-control."

Next, look for opportunities to practice using and to fortify the understanding of the question. Here is an example of character language integrated into classroom or everyday life: "Shannon, I hear you saying 'I can't!' You need a helper. You are a responsible person. Ask the Holy Spirit to be your helper." (In Chapter Eight, I will be discussing character language in detail.)

To further the experience, you could learn and teach a song about the Holy Spirit. An example of a song about the spirit of God is provided for you in Chapter Ten.

Principle 2: Attitudes Drive Actions

An attitude is an internal motivator behind a manner of acting that shows one's inward thoughts. For example, you might hear this statement: His friendly attitude showed his compassion for others. Scripture describes the relationship of attitude and mind: "to be made new in the attitude of your minds" (Ephesians 4:23b).

Scripture also talks about the relationship of attitudes and actions. "Your attitude should be the same as that of Christ Jesus: Who, being in very nature God,...made himself nothing.... And... humbled himself and became obedient to death—even death on a cross!" (Philippians 2:5–8). Attitudes determine the quality of one's life in relationship to others because they require choosing what is right or what is wrong. Because attitudes are abstract, educators and parents need to model, describe, label, and nurture them for children. Here is an example: "I like the way you ask questions about the story. Thank you for your curious attitude."

Take a moment and practice identifying a few attitudes. Following are four positive attitudes. Add four more to the list, and then briefly describe each attitude and one way to model it to a child.

Affirming   _____

Helpful   _____

Desiring to learn   _____

Curious   _____

One intervention I use to help children choose positive attitudes in the midst of a display of negative attitudes is the use of the character language phrase "attitude attack." Guided conversation in a situation might sound like this: "Jamie, I believe you are having an attitude attack. I understand, because we all have attitude attacks. You are choosing to be upset and sulk because it is story time and you wish to continue working with the play dough. But you are a responsible person, so find a stopping place, put your play dough in the plastic bag, and join the circle for story time. Thank you for choosing a helpful attitude."

Principal 3: Character Drives Conduct

Character is a collection of virtues and traits. The word *virtue* means good. I use the word *virtue* to describe "constructive character" and the word *trait* to describe "destructive character."

Here is a list of eight virtues and traits. Each virtue has an opposite, which is a trait. Remember that everyone receives character formation, just as everyone receives an education. The task is to intentionally form constructive character virtues in our children. Constructive virtues are antidotes to destructive traits.

> Constructive virtues are antidotes to destructive traits.

CONSTRUCTIVE CHARACTER VIRTUES		DESTRUCTIVE CHARACTER TRAITS
Compassion	....	Indifference
Forgiveness	....	Vengeance
Integrity	....	Dishonesty, Promise Breaking
Respect	....	Disdain (Scorn, Contempt)
Responsibility	....	Irresponsibility, Unwillingness to Commit
Initiative	....	Slothfulness, Laziness
Cooperation	....	Dissension, Opposition
Perseverance	....	Giving Up

Character virtues transform thoughts, attitudes, and actions inwardly. The inward transformation makes possible the outward transfer. Or, in other words, the logical result of character transformation is that the deeds of virtues such as compassion, forgiveness, integrity, respect, responsibility, initiative, cooperation, and perseverance flow naturally—and supernaturally in the likeness of Christ—to others.

Character virtues form the inner sense of what is right and wrong based on who a person is, not on laws or rules of conduct. Labeling something as right or wrong is vastly different from labeling it as good or bad. People are not good or bad. Chocolate is good, or it may taste bad. I am so discouraged when I hear an educator or parent say, "Run along now. That's a good boy" or "You are not listening. You are a bad girl."

It is actions and choices that are right or wrong. It is right to be considerate and respectful of others, to be responsible, to love, and to be generous. It is wrong to hit another person, to torment an animal, to think only of yourself, to lie, to steal, and to break promises. Choosing right inwardly may not show to the world, but it gives you the personal satisfaction of knowing you did the right thing and that you are a person of courage and reflect God's character. When others do notice your choice to do right, there is an added benefit. In author Mark Twain's words, "Always do right. This will gratify some people, and astonish the rest."

Character conduct is enhanced when those who serve children develop and consistently use habit structures. *Habit structures* are defined approaches/skills that become "habits" to ensure that you "habitually" employ chosen structures (e.g., modeling, giving example, using teachable moments, employing character language, and listening) in the classroom and everyday life.

Sterling Lands, in his book *The Main Ingredient*, tells us, "Habits are powerful factors in our lives. Because they are consistent, often unconscious patterns, they constantly express our character and produce our effectiveness or ineffectiveness."[3] Habit structures for children might include hanging up clothes, putting toys or video equipment away, and consistent use of the words *please* and *thank you*.

> Develop and consistently use habit structures.

Destructive or harmful habits such as selfishness, impatience, indifference, and revenge, to mention a few, can be broken. Forming a habit requires experiencing beliefs that drive positive behavior, attitudes that drive constructive actions, and character that drives conduct. Then compassion, forgiveness, integrity, respect, responsibility, initiative, cooperation, and perseverance become habitual.

NOTES

[1] Dallas Willard, *Renovation of the Heart* (Colorado Springs, CO: NavPress, 2002), 248.

[2] Robert Coles, *The Spiritual Life of Children* (Boston: Houghton Mifflin Company, 1990), 37.

[3] Sterling Lands II, *The Main Ingredient* (Austin, TX: Greater Calvary Publishing, 2002), 79.

Think on These Things

Beliefs drive behavior. What beliefs do you hold that drive your behavior relative to the virtue of integrity?

_____

_____

_____

What is one intentional way you can plan to be an example of this integrity belief and behavior for your children?

_____

_____

_____

Practice It!

List three habit structures that you would like to develop in your children relative to the virtue of responsibility. Okay, I'll give you the first one as an example.

1. _In any setting or situation, place trash in a trash container._
2. _____
3. _____

Read on. You are my heroes and heroines.

CHAPTER FOUR

Becoming People Who Live Out and Reflect God's Character

"You did not choose me, but I chose you and appointed you to go and bear fruit—fruit that will last."
John 15:16

"But the fruit of the Spirit is love, joy, peace, patience, kindness, goodness, faithfulness, gentleness and self-control. Against such things there is no law."
Galatians 5:22–23

How do individuals become people who live out and reflect God's character? Let's begin by considering what we are able to become as well as what we can do to guide the formation of godly character virtues in our children and a conscience that is able to discern right from wrong.

When I began to be intentional about character development, formation, and transformation, one of the questions that became important was, "How do I identify what are the basic virtues to be taught to all ages at all levels of learning?"

A rather obvious suggestion was offered to me by my team members: "Perhaps you need to look at God's basic character qualities, since what you want to develop in people is God's character."

Foundation Virtues and Family Virtues

As I was grappling with the suggestion to my question, I was privileged to be invited by Udo and Debbie Middelmann of the Francis A. Shaffer Foundation to come to their home for a week of study. The objective was to identify, through Scripture, the virtues that describe God's basic character. The result was the eight *foundation virtues* described in this book: compassion, forgiveness, integrity, respect, responsibility, initiative, cooperation, and perseverance.

After identifying these foundation virtues, we were able to identify and place other virtues that we believed could be developed in tandem with the development of each foundation virtue. These virtues we labeled *family virtues*. These family virtues develop and grow from the foundation virtues.

The foundation virtues are the larger concepts. For example, the foundation virtue of integrity includes truth, honesty, promise keeping, discernment, justice, and commitment, among others. In contrast, each family virtue is a smaller concept but an integral part of the foundation virtue.

Note in the chart that follows that there is a connectedness among these virtues. For instance, a virtue such as obedience develops and grows out of more than one foundation virtue. This connectedness is very important. I have discovered that when a virtue is presented to children apart from a foundation virtue, the results are often limited, shallow, or unbalanced. For example, when the virtue of obedience is developed from the foundation virtues of compassion, respect, and responsibility, the result is a broader, stronger, and more effective perspective of obedience than obedience as it relates to rules or laws alone.

FAMILY VIRTUES

COMPASSION
Love, Care, Kindness,
Self-Esteem, Self-Control,
Obedience, Promise Keeping,
Gentleness, Empathy, Trust,
Generosity, Sacrifice, Courage,
Justice

FORGIVENESS
Humility, Joy, Peace,
Mercy, Grace, Love,
Thankfulness, Gratitude,
Hope, Trust, Tenderness,
Justice

INTEGRITY
Truth, Honesty, Discernment,
Faithfulness, Trust, Wisdom,
Promise Keeping, Sincerity,
Commitment, Justice

RESPECT
Obedience, Patience,
Loyalty, Tolerance,
Courtesy, Honor, Encouragement

RESPONSIBILITY
Self-Discipline,
Self-Control, Dependability,
Obedience, Trust, Patience

INITIATIVE
Generosity, Courage,
Motivation, Boldness

COOPERATION
Authority, Generosity,
Goodness, Kindness, Humor

PERSEVERANCE
Endurance, Diligence,
Dependability, Loyalty,
Courage, Hope, Patience

To enhance your awareness of the strength and connectedness of foundation and family virtues, look at the chart again and find and circle the family virtue of trust within one of the eight foundation virtues. Then note the other three foundation virtues from which trust is developed and formed (forgiveness, integrity, and responsibility).

Approaches to Developing Character Virtues

Living successfully with others involves rules and precepts. Godly character development doesn't happen unintentionally. It requires good examples, instruction, and training (practice) in habits that affect thoughts, words, attitudes, actions, personality, and strength of character.

To become effective character builders, we need to first identify and define godly character virtues. Then we need to practice ways to apply and integrate the virtues into our lives. This same process may then be applied to the children we influence.

Godly character and conscience development is essentially the training of spirit and mind toward Christ. The developing of character virtues, therefore, requires the willingness of the learner and the teacher to enter into the process of becoming people who reflect God's character together.

Becoming people who reflect God's character is a process, and it involves

- instructing one's self and those you serve in what is right and what is wrong (beliefs drive behavior);
- nurturing the proper attitudes and actions first in one's self and then in others, so each wants to be and do right (attitudes drive actions);
- identifying, defining, applying, and integrating character virtues into all dimensions of life (character drives conduct).

Consider these three approaches to developing character virtues. They have proven to be very successful with various ages and across cultures.

1. Model/Example
   More character is "caught" rather than "taught." The modeling and living out of a character virtue in thoughts, words, attitudes, actions, and everyday experiences is essential. A woman accidentally knocks a can of soup off the shelf in

a grocery store. A mother has the opportunity to model to her child by picking up the can and replacing it on the shelf. As she does so, she intentionally remarks to her son, "Helping this lady is a right thing to do. It gives us a chance to practice being compassionate toward others."

2. Conflict/Choice

    The development of positive, godly character virtues is guided by using moments of conflict and decision to help children make constructive choices or learn from having made a poor choice. A child finds a five dollar bill on the school bus. He makes the choice to put it in his pocket. Later he tells his teacher that he found the money and kept it. The teacher asks him, "What would a person of integrity do with the five dollars?" Helping a child solve a problem at the moment it occurs is one of the most effective learning experiences. These moments are called "teachable moments" (more on teachable moments in Chapter Seven).

3. Intentional Strategies

    Intentional strategies are structured teaching experiences. It is important to determine the character virtue you wish to concentrate on for a defined length of time and then identify some measurable objectives and strategies to develop that character virtue. For example, in developing the character virtue of integrity, give children opportunities, appropriate to their maturity, to do the following:

    *   Talk about positive and negative experiences of the day. Reflecting upon something they wish they had done differently can be helpful in creating an open climate of honesty and discussion.
    *   Handle money for specific purposes. Think of opportunities for children to pay for sport or music tuitions and school lunches, give offerings at church or Sunday school, or purchase agreed upon clothing or games.

- <u>Have a special place for personal belongings</u>. A place for belongings gives children concrete boundaries to define what belongs to whom, which in turn defines the honesty required to not take or use what belongs to others.

- <u>Borrow and return items with owner's permission</u>. This opportunity allows a child to ask a favor of a friend and then be responsible in the handling and returning of the item in an agreed upon time.

- <u>Complete tasks in a mutually agreeable manner and time</u>. Label the task. Be specific ("Please put the building blocks away" or "Please stop the video game") and label the time ("Please find a stopping place to make it possible to leave here in fifteen minutes"). Be sure you are able to keep the task and time as well.

These opportunities are also concrete ways to introduce and develop the character virtue of responsibility. Being responsible is an act of integrity. A person of integrity is also a person of responsibility.

Here is another example of the use of an intentional strategy. Leading a group of third grade children in a worship experience included the receiving of their offering and then the taking of the collected offering across a courtyard to the office. Each time I would choose a different child to accomplish these tasks. Within this group of children was a young man who was a behavior challenge in many areas. I had observed that he needed opportunities to practice integrity and responsibility. I made the choice of giving him the opportunity to take the offering to the office, saying, "Eric, I know you are able to choose to be honest and responsible and deliver all this offering to the office."

The other children audibly responded with groans and comments of "no way," but I gave Eric eye contact and said, "I know you are able to make the right choice."

As Eric took the offering and walked across the courtyard, the other children moved to the window, saying things such as "he will never do it" and "watch him take some of the money out." But Eric did deliver all of the offering. His attitudes began to change as did the attitudes of the other children toward him.

As children begin to demonstrate character virtues, label their actions and give approval. Do so using the language of character. Here are some examples: "Thank you for telling me the truth." "Turning in the money you found is what a responsible person of integrity does. Thank you!"

Remember that character formation is first and foremost an inward transformation of spirit, mind, and conscience. Character formation can begin at any age. In the process of building character, a learner assumes responsibility within the self and lives out his or her own inward transformation. Transformed beliefs, attitudes, and character then transfer outward to others in changed thinking, words, attitudes, actions, and conscience.

Think on These Things

"Becoming people who live out and reflect God's character is a process of instructing one's self and those you serve in what is right and what is wrong. (Beliefs drive behavior.)"

Examine this statement, and then list some of what you define as right.

_____

_____

_____

Now list some of what you define as wrong.

_____

_____

_____

How do you know something is right or wrong? What is your basis of your standard?

_____

_____

_____

Practice It!

List one way you are teaching the children you serve to know right from wrong.

_____

_____

List one new way you plan to teach the children you serve to know right from wrong.

_____

_____

CHAPTER FIVE

Character Virtues: Definitions and Benefits to Society

"Be kind and compassionate to one another, forgiving each other just as in Christ God forgave you."
Ephesians 4:32

"Happy are people of integrity, who follow the law of the Lord."
Psalm 119:1 (NLT)

In this chapter, I want you to experience a sequence to help you more fully understand a character virtue in preparation for introducing and developing the virtue in your children.

As you experience the following sequence for three of the eight foundation virtues, I hope you will become aware of the importance for you, personally, to identify, explore, and wrestle with the forming of these virtues within yourself as well as within your children. When you are engaged in developing and forming God's character and being transformed into His likeness, God's purpose for becoming people who live out and reflect His character begins to become a reality.

Sequence for Understanding a Virtue

- define a virtue
- identify its benefits to society
- explore the Scripture basis for the virtue
- choose a story that illustrates the virtue
- determine which one of the three approaches the story uses (model/example, conflict/choice, or intentional strategy, as described in Chapter Four)
- discuss, label, and apply attitudes and actions illustrated in the story

God's book the Bible reveals to us God's character. First and foremost, He is a God of compassion, a God of forgiveness, and a God of integrity. These three character virtues are the most important of the eight foundation virtues. They are also the hardest to teach. Developing these three virtues first, in us and in our children, makes the developing of the other virtues an easier task.

If you are only able to introduce and begin the development of one virtue, I suggest that you choose compassion. Children respond to compassion and internalize compassion as it is given and modeled for them. Throughout Scripture we recognize God's continuous emphasis that the greatest character virtue is to be compassionate, loving, caring people. He is a compassionate God. His compassion never ends. His compassion is unconditional.

God's great compassion results in the giving of forgiveness. He loves so much that He gave His Son Jesus to make it possible for forgiveness. He is faithful and just to forgive. As a person becomes more compassionate, the virtue of forgiveness becomes a necessity.

Forgiveness is worth developing because of the need for people to forgive themselves and others and be freed from guilt and attitudes of failure. Forgiveness breaks the cycle of revenge that is so predominate in our culture. Forgiveness enhances compassion, and it requires integrity.

God is a God of integrity. He is the truth teller, does not lie, and always keeps His promises. Integrity is the larger concept that includes consistent sincerity, honesty, promise keeping, commitment, discernment, telling the truth, trust, faithfulness, wisdom, and justice. The void of integrity in our society requires us to model, be examples, and be very intentional in describing, teaching, and requiring integrity.

The character virtue definitions and benefits to society that I use in the following sequence have been crafted with input from many other leaders of character formation and transformation. You may wish to expand or edit them for your purpose and goals. *(At the end of this book in the Appendix, you will find definitions and benefits to society for the other five foundation virtues: respect, responsibility, initiative, cooperation, and perseverance.)*

Using the character virtue of compassion followed by forgiveness and integrity, you are going to experience a sequence to help you more fully understand any character virtue. The sequence serves as a model for one way you can prepare yourself to introduce to and develop these and other character virtues in your children.

Compassion

Begin with a clear definition of the character virtue. As the adult who is developing the virtue, your task is to make sure of your understanding of and ability to communicate the meaning of the virtue. The definition that you begin with, the one that is clear to you, needs to be one that also can be used with children.

Definition: Compassion is sympathy for someone else's suffering or misfortune, together with the desire to help, and appropriate action for his or her benefit.

Your definition may be re-worded for age-level appropriateness when working with younger children. Example: Compassion is a desire to help and care for others.

Be sure to keep it consistent, building on it, especially in teachable moments. "Carrie, your desire to help and care for others is a compassionate action. Thank you for including Tyler in the game."

Next identify the benefits to society of the virtue. The benefits to society are the logical consequences that may be expected as a result of belonging to a society of individuals who reflect the character virtue.

Benefits to society: All people want and need compassion. When people build relationships on compassion rather than power, they act to give to each other the best they have. Compassion allows people to bear all things, believe all things, hope all things, and endure all things.

A basic premise of this book is that character virtues are revealed in Scripture. So the next step is to identify Scriptures that describe and give meaning to the virtue. It is also helpful to read other authors who are expressing truths they have learned about the virtue.

> All people want and need compassion.

Scripture basis: "Jesus called his disciples to him and said, 'I have compassion for these people; they have already been with me three days and have nothing to eat. I do not want to send them away hungry, or they may collapse on the way'" (Matthew 15:32). In this Scripture, we see that Jesus lived out His inward compassion.

"[The Lord] crowns you with love and compassion" (Psalm 103:4).

Brennan Manning in his book *The Relentless Tenderness of Jesus* declares, "Before I can show compassion toward my brothers and sisters in their suffering, Jesus asks me to accept His compassion in my own life, to be transformed by it."[1] This inner transformation of the compassion of Jesus enables us to be compassionate toward ourselves, which in turns makes possible the outer transfer of compassion to others. Jesus is the model and His life the example of being compassionate and giving compassion.

Story: The next step in the sequence is to choose a story that exemplifies the virtue and then identify what approach is demonstrated in the story. Stories are one of the most effective ways to communicate the meaning and power of a virtue. Use them. Identifying the approach demonstrated in the story keeps you focused on repeating these effective methods.

Approach: The following story demonstrates the *model/example* approach. For children who think and learn concretely, the *model/example* approach is very effective in building their understanding of abstract concepts.

Five men were hurrying to catch their commuter train. As they hurried through the train station, they kicked over a table of apples that a boy had set up to sell so he could pay for his schooling. One of the men felt guilty and said to the others, "Go ahead, I need to stop." He went back to the boy. "How old are you?" he asked. "I'm ten years old, sir." Only then did the man realize that this boy was blind. "Here," he said, "is $20 to pay for the apples we spoiled. I must hurry on and catch up with my friends." The blind boy called after him, "Wait a minute, sir. Are you Jesus?"

Discussion, labeling, and application: At the end of the story, the boy asked the question, "Are you Jesus?" What generated his question? Hopefully your conclusion is that the man's compassion generated the question. Notice that the boy learned about compassion through the man's *model/example*, which he correctly associated with Jesus.

For younger children, the question to ask after telling the story might be, "Why did the boy ask the question, 'Are you Jesus'?"

You have just experienced the basic sequence to begin the development and formation of a character virtue: definition; benefits to society; Scriptures; story; approach; and discussion, labeling, and application of attitudes and actions found in the story.

As you continue to develop this character virtue with your children, you can tell more compassion stories or have a few sessions or lessons with the main focus on compassion. But remember that the development of compassion is enhanced when you fortify its development with one or more of its family virtues. So, look again at the family virtue visual.

FAMILY VIRTUES

COMPASSION
Love, Care, Kindness,
Self-Esteem, Self-Control,
Obedience, Promise Keeping,
Gentleness, Empathy, Trust,
Generosity, Sacrifice, Courage,
Justice

FORGIVENESS
Humility, Joy, Peace,
Mercy, Grace, Love,
Thankfulness, Gratitude,
Hope, Trust, Tenderness,
Justice

INTEGRITY
Truth, Honesty, Discernment,
Faithfulness, Trust, Wisdom,
Promise Keeping, Sincerity,
Commitment, Justice

RESPECT
Obedience, Patience,
Loyalty, Tolerance,
Courtesy, Honor, Encouragement

RESPONSIBILITY
Self-Discipline,
Self-Control, Dependability,
Obedience, Trust, Patience

INITIATIVE
Generosity, Courage,
Motivation, Boldness

COOPERATION
Authority, Generosity,
Goodness, Kindness, Humor

PERSEVERANCE
Endurance, Diligence,
Dependability, Loyalty,
Courage, Hope, Patience

Which of the family virtues flowing from the foundation virtue of compassion catches your attention?

Let's say it is love. Now do some fortification of the family virtue of love by going through the same sequence you just did with compassion: definition; benefits to society (most likely the benefits to society will be the same as those identified for compassion); Scriptures (1 John 4:19 says, "We love because he first loved us."); a story (one that focuses on love but also makes it possible for you to label compassionate attitudes and actions); approach; and then discussion, labeling, and application of the actions and attitudes in the story.

Next you might introduce the family virtue of trust. It is a truth that for many of us trust does not come easily. Ultimately we trust God because He loves us and we love Him. Brennan Manning puts it this way: "You will trust God only as much as you love Him. And you will love Him not because you have studied Him; you will love Him because you have touched Him—in response to His touch."[2]

Can you see how logical and effective it is to first teach compassion, then love, and then trust?

Forgiveness

Definition: Forgiveness means to no longer blame or be angry with someone who has hurt or wronged you, including yourself. Forgiveness is to pardon or excuse a wrong thought, word, attitude, or action without condition.

Benefits to society: When people practice forgiveness in the community, they break the cycle of revenge. When a person experiences forgiveness, he or she is freed from guilt and attitudes of failure. When people sense they have failed, they lose their productivity. When people receive forgiveness, they regain their motivation to contribute to society.

Scripture basis: "Love your enemies, and do good to them... and you will be the sons of the Most High, because he is kind to the ungrateful and wicked" (Luke 6:35). Notice that this Scripture points to an intimate connection between compassion and forgiveness.

"If you forgive others their trespasses, your heavenly Father will also forgive you" (Matthew 6:14, NRSV).

"Bear with each other and forgive whatever grievances you may have against one another. Forgive as the Lord forgave you" (Colossians 3:13).

Story and approach: This story, as told by Corrie ten Boom, demonstrates the *intentional strategies* approach to present the virtue of forgiveness.

It was in a church in Munich that I saw him—a balding, heavyset man in a gray overcoat, a brown felt hat clutched between his hands. People were filing out of the basement room where I had just spoken. It was 1947 and I had come from Holland to defeated Germany with the message that God forgives.

"When we confess our sins," I had said, "God casts them into the deepest ocean, gone forever."

The place was Ravensbruck and the man moving towards me had been one of the cruelest guards. Now he was in front of me, hand thrust out: "A fine message, Fraulein! How good it is to know that, as you say, all our sins are at the bottom of the sea!" And I, who had spoken so glibly of forgiveness, fumbled in my pocketbook rather than take that hand.

"You mentioned Ravensbruck in your talk," he was saying. "I was a guard there. But since that time, I have become a Christian. I know that God has forgiven me for the cruel things I did there, but I would like to hear it from your lips as well. Fraulein,"—again the hand came out—"will you forgive me?"

It could not have been many seconds that he stood there—hand held out—but to me it seemed hours as I wrestled with the most difficult thing I had ever had to do. Mechanically yet intentionally, I thrust my hand into the one stretched out to me. And as I did, an incredible thing took place. The current started in my shoulder, raced down my arm, sprang into our joined hands. And then this healing warmth seemed to flood my whole being, bringing tears to my eyes.

"I forgive you, brother!" I cried. "With all my heart."[3]

Discussion, labeling, and application: Forgiveness brings healing to the forgiver. Forgiveness breaks the cycle of revenge. A question for elementary age children might be, "When did Corrie realize she had not forgiven those who were so cruel to her while she was in the Ravensbruck concentration camp?" Emphasize that Corrie had to make an intentional decision to forgive.

You now have completed the basic sequence with the virtue of forgiveness. Once again, you may want to continue the developing of this virtue by having a few more stories, sessions, or lessons with the main focus on forgiveness, but the best way to fortify the development of forgiveness at this point is to introduce and develop understanding of one or more of its family virtues. So, look

> Forgiveness breaks the cycle of revenge.

back at the family virtues visual. Which of the family virtues flowing from the foundation virtue of forgiveness catches your attention? It might be that you wish to continue to build with the virtues of love and trust.

Now I am taking you through the same practice of the sequence one more time, this time with the virtue of integrity.

Integrity

Definition: Integrity is strength and firmness of character that results in consistent sincerity and honesty. People of integrity keep their word.

Benefits to society: Many systems of law and justice are based upon the Bible. These teachings provide an absolute standard for integrity so that society can determine whether the action of an individual is acceptable or not. An absolute standard keeps corrupt leaders from making one law for the people and another law for themselves. As people act with integrity, integrity is infused into society, bringing maximum value to the law.

Scripture basis: "In everything...show integrity, seriousness and soundness of speech" (Titus 2:7).

> As people act with integrity, integrity is infused into society, bringing maximum value to the law.

Story and approach: A referee tells of a well played and closely contested championship high school basketball game between New Rochelle and Yonkers High. This story demonstrates the *conflict/choice* approach and presents the virtue of integrity.

Yonkers was leading by one point as I glanced at the clock, to discover only 30 seconds left to play.

Yonkers, in possession of the ball, shot and missed. New Rochelle recovered, pushed the ball up court, shot, but the ball rolled tantalizingly around the rim and off.

New Rochelle, the home team, got the rebound and tapped it in for what looked like victory. I glanced at the clock. The game was over, but I hadn't heard the final buzzer because of the noise of the crowd.

I approached the timekeeper, a young man of 17 or so. He said that the buzzer went off as the ball rolled off the rim, before the final tap-in was made.

I had to tell the home team coach that time had run out before the final basket was tapped in. Yonkers had won the game. The coach's face clouded over. As the young timekeeper joined us he said, "I'm sorry, Dad. The time ran out before the final basket."

Suddenly, the coach's face lit up. He said, "That's OK, Joe. You were honest and right. You told the truth. I'm proud of you." Turning to me, he said, "Al, I want you to meet my son, Joe."[4]

Discussion, labeling, and application: Notice the conflict/choice here that Joe faces over telling his dad the truth. Questions to ask children after telling this story would be, "What was Joe's conflict? What choices did Joe have? What choice did Joe make?" Joe's dad had a choice to make as well. He chose to encourage his son to be a person of integrity, to be honest and tell the truth.

Again the basic sequence is completed, and now is the time to decide to have a few more stories, sessions, or lessons with the main focus on integrity or to fortify the development of integrity with its family virtues. Look again at the family virtue chart. There is the opportunity to continue building trust as well as introducing one or two other virtues that are best for your children.

The developing of integrity challenges us to trust and discern what is being formed in the children we are serving. Listen to the story of a five-year-old girl I will call Kali, who attended a preschool in a Texas community where integrity was the focus of their character formation.

One day at her home, as Kali entered the bathroom, she saw a snake curled up in the open wire trash basket. Kali ran to her mother, shouting, "There is a snake in the bathroom! Come quickly!" They raced to the bathroom, only to discover that there was no snake. But Kali insisted she had seen a snake and went crying to her room.

Later that afternoon, her old brother marched into the family room holding a small garter snake. "I found him in my bedroom," he said.

"Oh, Kali, I apologize," her mother said. "This must be the snake you saw."

Kali replied, "See Mom, I do tell the truth. I am a person of integrity."

When we have done something wrong or are worried about what others may think, we tend to fear the telling of the truth, and yet Jesus said, "I came into the world to bring everything into the clear light of day, making all the distinctions clear, so that those who have never seen will see, and those who have made a great pretense of seeing will be exposed as blind" (John 9:39, msg). In John 8:31 (msg), Jesus says, "If you stick with this, living out what I tell you, you are my disciples for sure. Then you will experience for yourselves the truth, and the truth will free you." These Scriptures tell us that integrity gives light and freedom to our lives.

Developing Character Virtues as Adults

It is important for us as adults, parents, teachers, coaches, and other influencers of children to become aware of our own inward transformation possibilities and needs. This personal awareness, I believe, is essential to the effectiveness of guiding children's character formation.

To what extent have the foundation character virtues of compassion, forgiveness, and integrity been formed in us as adults? What about the family virtues? It behooves each of us who serve children to examine ourselves. It is not too late to memorize and internalize Scripture in order to live out and transfer a set of beliefs (worldview) that reflect Jesus and His Father's character.

Think with me about the virtue of integrity. It is good for those of us who desire to develop the virtue of integrity in ourselves and our children to examine some of the truths we may or may not know about ourselves and the world in which we live if we are followers of the Lord Jesus of the Bible. Here are three.

1. It is a broken world. Brennan Manning says, "We are broken people. Our brokenness reveals something about who we are. Our brokenness is lived and experienced as highly personal, intimate and unique. When I get honest, I admit I am a bundle of paradoxes. I believe and I doubt, I hope and I get discouraged, I love and I hate, I feel bad about feeling good, I feel guilty about not feeling guilty. I am trusting and suspicious, I am honest and I still play games."[5]

2. We are the beloved sons and daughters of God. The leaders and prophets of Israel as well as the apostles of the New Testament all to one degree or another lived broken lives. We cannot escape our brokenness either. It is true that we not only are "the Beloved" but we are becoming "the Beloved." Becoming "the Beloved" means letting the truth of God's compassionate character and unconditional love become a part of the commonplaces of our everyday lives. It needs to become a part of everything we think, say, and do.

3. We belong to the Father of Jesus. We are able to resist a broken world filled with voices that shout, "You are no good, you are ugly, you are worthless, and you are nobody," because God calls us His Beloved.

    Henry Nouwen says, "The greatest lie and trap in our life is not success, popularity, or power, but self-rejection. Self-rejection is the darkness of not feeling truly welcome in human existence. It is the greatest enemy of the spiritual life because it contradicts God's truth, God's voice that calls us the 'Beloved.' Being the Beloved expresses the core truth of our existence."[6]

NOTES

[1] Brennan Manning, *The Relentless Tenderness of Jesus* (Grand Rapids, MI: Fleming H. Revell Co., 2004), 70.

[2] Ibid., 74.

[3] Corrie ten Boom, "I'm Still Learning to Forgive," *Guideposts Magazine* (1972).

[4] Al Covino, "Winners and Winners," *A 4th Course of Chicken Soup for the Soul: 101 Stories to Open the Heart and Rekindle the Spirit,* ed. Jack Canfield, Mark Victor Hansen, Hanoch McCarty and Meladee McCarty (Deerfield Beach, FL: Health Communications, Inc., 1997).

[5] Brennan Manning, *Reflections for Ragamuffins: Daily Devotions from the Writings of Brennan Manning* (San Francisco, CA: Harper, 1998), 21.

[6] Henri J.M. Nouwen, *Life of the Beloved* (NY: Crossroad Publishing, 1992), 27.

Think on These Things

Please look back at the family virtue chart. What family virtues do you find listed under compassion and forgiveness that are common to both?

_____
_____
_____

What is the benefit of developing compassion and forgiveness in tandem with trust?

_____
_____
_____

How does the referee story demonstrate a teachable moment of choice and conflict in regard to integrity?

_____
_____
_____

Practice It!

Choose and list one story that you are familiar with that demonstrates each of the following virtues. Be sure it is appropriate for the age of the children you are serving.

Compassion _____
Forgiveness _____
Integrity _____

Then determine which one of the three approaches the story uses (model/example, conflict/choice, or intentional strategy, as described in Chapter Four).

(Some age-appropriate stories may be found in the Appendix.)

CHAPTER SIX

Character Virtues Develop Transformed Values

"I rejoice in following your statutes as one rejoices in great riches."
Psalm 119:14

The previous chapter introduced a sequence for the process of understanding character virtues. It is also important for us and the children we serve to understand the relationship of character to worldview and values. We need to understand how character virtues, biblical worldview, and resulting values transform us inwardly. And, we need to recognize how to live them out and transfer them to others in our everyday, walk-around lives.

When I was five years old, my family lived on a block that had three houses located in the middle of the block. On the south end of the block was a restaurant with a parking lot, and on the north end there were three business establishments with a square walkway in front of them. My house was the middle house. I was allowed to ride my tricycle to the south only as far as where the parking lot began, but I could go all the way to the north and ride around the square walkway and back to my house. Mr. and Mrs. Black were the owners of the drugstore that sat on the corner. They knew my family and me by name. I would often ride my tricycle down, go in to the store, and just say hi.

One day I saw a display of Hershey almond chocolate bars. As I went by it, I was sure I heard a chocolate bar say, "Take me." I said hello to Mr. and Mrs. Black, and as I passed the display, I took a Hershey bar. I jumped on my tricycle, road to my house, went around to the back porch, opened the candy, and enjoyed eating the whole bar. I then heard the phone ring. My grandmother answered. "Well, hello Mr. Black. How nice to hear from you." Oh my, I knew right away why Mr. Black was calling. Grandma's next words were, "Verneal (that's my full name) will be right down, Mr. Black. Thank you for calling."

My grandma sat down beside me and told me that Mr. Black had seen me take the candy bar. She said, "Mr. Black and I both care for you too much to let you become a person who steals from others." I began to cry and tell my grandma how sorry I was for taking the candy. She replied, "It is wrong to take something without paying for it. But Mr. Black will let you make it right by talking to him and paying him for the candy bar."

Grandma wiped my tears, helped me take the correct amount of money out of my piggy bank, and walked me to the front door. "You're coming with me, aren't you, Grandma?" "No, Verneal," she replied. "You took the candy bar by yourself, you ate it by yourself, and now you can make this right by yourself. I will stand right here and watch if you need help, and I will be right here when you come back to hug and thank you for doing what is right."

My grandma's character, worldview, and values were dramatically acted out before me.

Developing the spiritual life, character, and conscience of children requires a framework, an overarching guideline, a worldview upon which standards and truths are tested. The content of this book and its author (that's me) hold a worldview based on God's character, biblical principles, and transformed values that reflect the attitudes and actions of Christ Jesus. God loves us and knows what we can become. He is a gentle and kind transformer who gives us life.

This chapter will help you see your worldview more clearly and give you tips on how you can help shape the worldview of your children. It will help you become aware of the character formation that takes place in you when you understand and begin to live out the foundation virtues, their family virtues, and the set of transformed values that are a result.

Biblical Worldview

A biblical worldview is radically different from other worldviews. A *biblical worldview* is a set of beliefs that hold the truths that the Bible relates to all of life. The Bible is the book that unifies

> *A biblical worldview* is a set of beliefs that hold the truths that the Bible relates to all of life.

and articulates the ways of God both through history and as revealed through the actions and words of His Son Jesus. The forming of a biblical worldview asks people to use the Bible and their minds to discover what is the truth of the universe.

The developing of a biblical worldview starts when people are willing to search for (and therefore deserve) honest answers. Udo Middelmann, president of the Francis A. Schaeffer Foundation and author of *The Market Driven Church,* describes the first step in this way: "It is not where I start that is important, but where I end up: concluding that what the Bible talks about is, indeed, true. The Bible gives me the answers I require if I am honest as a person in real history."[1]

An honest study of the Scripture leads to this set of biblical conclusions:

- What the Bible talks about is true.
- There is an eternal Person who feels and thinks.
- This person is God, who made energy and who made human beings in His image.
- God is a personal creator. He created each of us individually; therefore, there is a purpose to our individual existence.
- He comes to us in Jesus Christ, whom we can totally trust.
- We live in a moral universe where right and wrong are clearly defined by God. Right and wrong are not imposed by power. Right and wrong have to do with the kind of

world God has made. To break the laws of right and wrong is not only to violate God's feelings and character, but it is to do something utterly destructive and foolish.

- We live in a rational, ordered universe. The sun continues to give us light each day, and the moon follows its twenty-eight day cycle. The earth stays on its axis and continues to rotate so that we have day and night. The earth continues to go around the sun every year, which gives us seasons that remain constant: summer, fall, winter, and spring.

- We are created to be human beings with minds and hands, to be used to nourish body and soul as well as to have dominion over nature and to create the flow of history in a deliberate use of culture over nature.

- The big picture of life for every age can only be explained to human beings through a revelation from God, set in text and language that addresses the mind and deals with real life issues. Questions are not to be squashed, and answers need to be examined for their truthfulness.

Character Formation and a Biblical Worldview

Character formation based on a biblical worldview is an ongoing, lifetime process. Being aware of your present worldview and the ongoing, lifetime process of character formation is integral to your understanding of the progression from character virtues to a set of transformed values. The character formation that takes place in us when we understand and begin to live out the foundation virtues and their family virtues results in a set of transformed values.

PROGRESSION FROM CHARACTER VIRTUES TO VALUES

FOUNDATION CHARACTER VIRTUE ⇨	FAMILY VIRTUES ⇨	TRANSFORMED VALUES= WORLDVIEW REFLECTING GOD AND HIS SON, JESUS
COMPASSION	Love Self-Esteem/Self-Control Care Promise Keeping Gentleness, Empathy Sacrifice	Love-driven obedience Positive personal commitment Compassion for and care of others Promised love lived out Dependence upon God
FORGIVENESS	Humility Gratitude Joy, Peace Grace, Mercy	Restoration Serving others Reconciliation Tenderness
INTEGRITY	Truth Honesty Discernment, Wisdom Trust Justice Faithfulness	Setting people free Equity Focusing on what matters most Choosing to build trust
RESPECT	Courtesy Honor Loyalty Encouragement	Respect for self and others Honoring others through listening, speech, and action Faithful to family, friends, and lawful government
RESPONSIBILITY	Self-Discipline Dependability Obedience	Solving problems through conscience and consequence Accountability for individual behavior Choosing to obey righteous authority
INITIATIVE	Generosity Courage Motivation Boldness	Unprompted action Risk taking Internal motivation

COOPERATION	Goodness	Support for ideas of others
	Kindness	Respect for another's
	Humor	uniqueness
	Tolerance	Sprinkling challenges with
		humor
		Negotiating
PERSEVERANCE	Endurance	Never giving up
	Hope	Being patient with self
	Patience	Concentrated commitment
	Diligence	

Let's consider, as an example, the character formation progression from the foundation virtue of compassion and its family virtues that results in a set of transformed values.

PROGRESSION FROM CHARACTER VIRTUES TO VALUES

FOUNDATION CHARACTER VIRTUE ⇨	FAMILY VIRTUES ⇨	TRANSFORMED VALUES= WORLDVIEW REFLECTING GOD AND HIS SON, JESUS
COMPASSION	Love	Love-driven obedience
COMPASSION	Self-Esteem	Positive personal commitment
COMPASSION	Self-Control	
COMPASSION	Care	Concern and care of others

Please remember that the formation of character is not behavior modification. Character formation develops beliefs that drive behavior, attitudes that drive actions, and character virtues that drive the conduct and conscience of persons who reflect God's character. In other words, the forming of God's character within us produces a belief system, a worldview that reflects the ways of Jesus and the character of His Father and our Father God.

Think with me for a moment. What are some elements of character and values that you see in our culture today? List your thoughts here, placing what you believe are constructive and what you believe are destructive.

Constructive: Destructive:

_____   _____

_____   _____

_____   _____

_____   _____

Compare your list to the following list that was presented in Chapter Three.

CONSTRUCTIVE CHARACTER VIRTUES	DESTRUCTIVE CHARACTER TRAITS
Compassion	Indifference
Forgiveness	Vengeance
Integrity	Dishonesty, Promise Breaking
Respect	Disdain (Scorn, Contempt)
Responsibility	Irresponsibility, Unwillingness to Commit
Initiative	Slothfulness, Laziness
Cooperation	Dissension, Opposition
Perseverance	Giving Up

The positive character virtues and values that reflect God and His Son Jesus don't just appear in us as a result of being born. Contrary to popular thought, basic goodness is not something people naturally possess. We all can observe both positive virtues and negative traits in the children we serve. Our ongoing task, then, is to fortify positive virtues and redirect when children demonstrate negative traits. By doing so, we are helping our children in the formation of positive character, a biblical worldview, and values that reflect God's character.

When a preschooler demands attention or grabs a toy, we need to be intentional about modeling, labeling, and guiding the child to be gentle. When a child declares, "I give up," we need to be intentional about modeling, labeling, and guiding the child to persevere and never, never give up. If we do nothing to model or live out positive character virtues, we are actually reinforcing the negative character traits. Virtues, therefore, are the antidote, or correction, to the negative traits.

When you observe an attitude or act of indifference in a child toward others, redirect the child to an attitude or act of compassion. Here is an example of putting this principle into practice in your everyday life. You see your child run and bump into a woman in a store, causing her to drop her packages. Your child just keeps running. Use this teachable moment to redirect your child to help the woman pick up her packages and apologize.

Ten Big Ideas on Developing Character in Children

Here are ten big ideas on developing character in children.

1. Be aware that children develop character slowly and in stages.
2. Teach and develop character by example.
3. Provide ways for children to make choices.
4. Love children. Love is vital for character development, formation, and transformation.
5. Initiate and demonstrate forgiveness.
6. Help children learn to think with discernment and honesty.
7. Respect children, and require respect in return.
8. Help children assume real responsibilities.
9. Ask questions instead of giving answers.
10. Balance high support and high control.

The challenge is before us—to be people who live out and reflect God's character and who develop people who live out and reflect God's character. Here is a pledge that I encourage children, youth, parents, guides, and teachers to memorize:

We pledge to continue to strive to be people who live out and reflect God's character, being and doing...

- the right thing,
- the right way,
- for the right reason,
- expecting the right result,
- to benefit others and glorify God,
- according to God's book the Bible[2]

The logical consequence of developing people who live out and reflect God's character is character-driven people who continue to form a biblical worldview and values that reflect God's statutes and character. Never give up developing and correcting your own and your learners' worldviews with the reality and truth of God's character and ways.

NOTES

[1] Udo W. Middelmann, *The Market Driven Church* (Wheaton, IL: Crossway Books, 2004).

[2] Adapted from ANAK Consultants, Austin, TX.

Think on These Things

Choose one of the eight foundation virtues you wish to consider more fully. Write that virtue here. _____

Write the family virtue you choose to develop more fully as you think on the foundation virtue you listed. _____

Practice It!

Choose one of the ten big ideas that you can intentionally put into practice in relationship to the virtues you have chosen, first in yourself and then with your child(ren). Write your choice here. _____

_____

_____

_____

Record your progress over the next several days.

_____

_____

_____

_____

_____

_____

_____

CHAPTER SEVEN

How Children Think and Learn

"Lord, tell me your ways. Show me how to live.
Guide me in your truth."
Psalm 25:4–5a (ICB)

It is imperative to the growth of children's spiritual life and the formation of their character and conscience for us to understand how children think and learn.

If we desire the most effective learning and transformation of character and conscience in our children, we must be aware of all areas of child development. Each area has its own needs. Our planning of learning experiences must take into consideration how the needs in each area are to be met.

This illustration shows the five areas of child development: intellectual, physical, emotional, social, and spiritual. All areas affect and interact with one

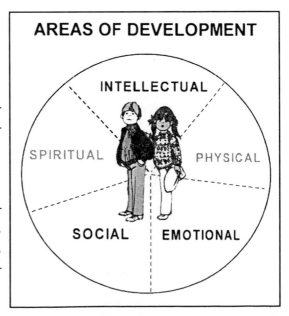

AREAS OF DEVELOPMENT

INTELLECTUAL

SPIRITUAL

PHYSICAL

SOCIAL

EMOTIONAL

another. The learning experiences we create, therefore, need to involve the total child if we are to avoid fragmented learning.

Take a moment to jot down what you understand about each area. With which area are you the least familiar?

Often the area of spiritual development is skipped over or, for various reasons, ignored. Perhaps this is true because parents and teachers have not experienced being taught about their spiritual life. Or there may be hesitancy for lack of understanding on how to create concrete learning experiences for abstract ideas.

The formation of character and conscience is a primary aspect of a child's spiritual development. Spiritual development is directly related to a child's stage of intellectual development. Children's intellectual development is in what educators label as the concrete stage. Therefore, since their spiritual development is directly related to their intellectual development, children's spiritual development also is occurring primarily in the concrete stage.

Concrete experiences form the basic structure of early childhood and children's thinking. Concrete experiences are those that allow children to use their five senses of touch, taste, sight, sound, and smell to assimilate concepts.

As we consider ways to talk with children about their spiritual lives and character formation, it is important to understand how children can become confused. Here are three principles that limit their ability to think clearly about abstract concepts.

Principle One:
Children's thinking is limited by their perspective.

Often when we teach children about who God is, we talk about God as "our Father." We want to communicate that God's love never changes, that He consistently forgives us, that He is always there for us, and that He desires to be intimate with us. The problem occurs when we talk about God in this way to a child whose human father is abusive, alcoholic, neglectful, or absent. Because of this child's limited life experience, his or her perspective of "father" is different (even opposite) from what we are trying to communicate about God.

As we begin effectively teaching this child about God, His character, and life with God, it is important to find and use some other concrete realities about God such as a rainbow, the sun, stars, or beautiful
trees covered with snow. A teacher or parent might ask, for example,
"What does a rainbow tell us about God?" and then connect the idea to
the child with the comment, "God creates beautifully and wonderfully.
He created you the same way. His rainbow tells us that God is with us
here and now."

Not only is children's thinking limited by their perspective, but
their perspective is limited because they have a tendency to focus
attention on secondary, or nonessen-
tial, aspects of a situation. Here's an
example: A teacher was telling the
story of Jesus being arrested by sol-
diers. He mentioned that the sol-
diers had swords. One boy interrupt-

> Children's perspective is lim-
> ited because they have a ten-
> dency to focus attention on
> secondary, or non-essential,
> aspects of a situation.

ed and began talking about the new toy sword he had received for
his birthday. The child had fastened his attention on the secondary,
or nonessential, part of the story that was familiar and important
to him.

A perceptive teacher or parent who understands this principle of
a child's limited perspective might respond by saying something like,
"Bobby, I can tell how excited you are about your new toy sword. You
may imagine that you have your sword while you listen to what happened to the people in our Bible story."

Related to a child's inability to focus on the significant portions of
a situation is the ease with which children can give correct answers that
are, in fact, meaningless to them. For instance, upon hearing a story of
a grandmother who forgave her granddaughter for telling a lie, a group
of children was asked, "Why wasn't the grandmother angry and want-
ing to punish the granddaughter for doing wrong instead of being kind
and forgiving?" One child replied, "Because the granddaughter said
she was sorry, so the grandmother had to forgive her." The teacher then
asked, "What does it mean to forgive someone?" The child shrugged
his shoulders and could not respond.

A wise teacher or parent who understands the limitation of this
child's perspective might respond by beginning with the part of for-

giveness a child is most familiar with: "Forgiveness is more than saying 'I'm sorry.' Forgiveness begins when you agree with God that what you thought, said, or did is something God does not want people to think, say, or do." The teacher or parent can then say, "Forgiveness includes telling the person you hurt that what you thought, said, or did is wrong. Forgiveness also includes giving and receiving kindness and love. God's book the Bible says, 'Make sure that nobody pays back wrong for wrong, but always try to be kind to each other and to everyone else.'"

> Forgiveness is more than saying "I'm sorry." Forgiveness begins when you agree with God that what you thought, said, or did is something God does not want people to think, say, or do.

Children's perspective is also limited because they are capable of repeating words even though what they are repeating is totally meaningless to them. Children can repeat words that are expected of them by adults, give correct answers they have learned to give, and receive praise from adults, all the while not understanding what the words mean. We must take care to see that what children say is not just repetition but is meaningful to them. This can be accomplished by careful listening and asking open-ended questions.

> Children's perspective is also limited because they are capable of repeating words even though what they are repeating is totally meaningless to them.

Not long ago I was visiting a young child in her home. Her parents were so excited for me to hear that their five-year-old had memorized the twenty-third Psalm. After the child repeated all of the verses from memory, I asked, "What parts of these words do you like the most?" "I don't really know," she responded, "but I don't want to lie down in a green pasture."

Often a great deal of misunderstanding occurs in a child's thinking because children incorrectly interpret abstract terms to fit their concrete thinking. Some adults think of these misunderstandings as humorous. And they are. But more important is that they are a clue to those who listen that the child is thinking concretely. Listen to this conversation. Five-year-old Justin is sitting in church, keeping busy by singing and talking. His seven-year-old sister tells him to stop. Justin answers, "Why? Who's going to make me?" Justin's sister says, "See those men holding the bulletins? They are called 'hushers.'"

As leaders, teachers, and parents, we have the opportunity to listen and then with gentle kindness lead the child to the correct understanding: "The name of the people holding bulletins is 'usher.' To usher means to help people by giving them a bulletin and perhaps find them a place to sit. The name usher sure sounds like 'husher.'"

What is abstract thinking? It is the ability to think about abstract relationships and symbolism, to formulate hypotheses, and to consider possibilities and abstractions like forgiveness. Previous studies have shown that the ability to think abstractly begins around the age of eleven or twelve. More recent studies, however, have shown that abstract thinking does not begin until age thirteen and, in many teens, much later. According to Jean Piaget[1], many adults never fully develop this ability to think abstractly, also known as formally. It is not an ability that suddenly appears at age thirteen. For this reason, it is so important to give children opportunities to think and talk about both concrete and abstract ideas.

Think again about children's perspective of forgiveness, which is an abstract concept. Their perspective is often incorrectly formed because they are taught forgiveness by someone saying to them, "Forgive your friend and say that you are sorry." In reality, saying "I am sorry" is repentance, not forgiveness. Remember, forgiveness begins when a person agrees with God that he or she has thought, said, or done something God does not want people to think about, say, or do. For children, forgiveness starts with agreeing with a significant adult in their life or the authority figure in a situation that a wrong has occurred.

We adults can then guide children to say, "I'm wrong" and then, "I'm sorry." It is usually easy for a child to say, "I'm sorry," but often children are initially unwilling to admit that they are wrong. An indication of the desired inward transformation might be the child's ability to say, "I'm wrong."

Principle Two:
Children's thinking depends on the quality and quantity of firsthand experiences.

Because children think concretely, firsthand experiences give them opportunities to use their five senses to gain understanding. When an adult wants a child to experience an abstract concept such as kindness, the adult needs to create or take advantage of a quality firsthand experience that demonstrates kindness. For example, nine-year-old David's teacher or parent may take advantage of a time when she or he sees David being kind to his friend by saying, "David, giving your book to Raul was a kind thing to do." Creating a firsthand experience might include asking children to do something kind: "Stefanie, would you please do me a kindness by holding the door open for me?"

Increasing the quantity and quality of firsthand experiences occurs as leaders, teachers, and parents make a habit to continuously watch for, label, and describe firsthand experiences. Wise leaders, teachers, and parents look for everyday opportunities. "Thank you for inviting Tammy to sit next to you. The invitation was a kind thing to do." "Slowing down and allowing the older gentlemen to enter the store first tells me you are thinking of others. You are becoming a compassionate person."

> Increasing the quantity and quality of firsthand experiences occurs as leaders, teachers, and parents make a habit to continuously watch for, label, and describe firsthand experiences.

Principle Three:
Children's thinking is limited to physical activities.

Besides having the limitations of perspective and the need for firsthand experiences, a child's mental development requires physical objects to manipulate. An abstract idea such as trust, for example, needs to be recast in physical experiences to enable children to attach meaning to the abstract concept.

> A child's mental development requires physical objects to manipulate.

Creating a physical experience for trust may be as simple as having children experience a trust walk. In a trust walk, children are paired. One child is blindfolded, and the other is not. The blindfolded child is led safely around simple objects by the other child. The blindfolded child experiences trust, while the other child experiences being a trustworthy guide. In conversation afterward, the children are asked to describe what attitude was needed to trust and what attitude was needed to be trustworthy.

When we keep these three principles as primary guidelines in working with children, we allow children to explore and grow their "with-God life," their spiritual life, in the best and most personal way. The phrase "with-God life" is used with children at the earliest ages to grow the truth that God is with them here and now.

> The phrase "with-God life" is used with children at the earliest ages to grow the truth that God is with them here and now.

Critical Thinking

Having identified how children think and learn, we can now focus on ways to develop their critical thinking. Before you read on, ponder these four questions to help you determine where you are in your understanding of critical thinking.

1. What does the term *critical thinking* mean to you?
2. Why is it important to teach children to "think critically"?
3. What happens when people don't think critically?
4. Who has taught or will teach you to think critically?

I am concerned about some of the ways in which children are being taught to think. Many teachers, parents, and coaches teach from the perspective that learning is all about facts—knowing stories, memorizing data, and having certain answers to certain questions. Following are two illustrations.

When eight-year-old Thomas was asked what he thought about his Sunday school experience, he replied, "I don't need to think in this class. All I need to do when I'm asked a question is to answer yes, no, Jesus, or God."

When eleven-year-old Stefani was asked why she didn't like her language arts class, she said, "We've done all this before, and I don't have to think or respond with any ideas but the teacher's."

What is the purpose of education? Is it to teach reading, writing, math, science, social studies, geography, spelling, art, music, facts, and skills? Or is the purpose to prepare individuals to become responsible members of society—members who are not only proficient in these areas but also who think critically, live out positive character virtues, and have a conscience to choose right over wrong?

If the answer is skills plus members of society plus positive character virtues and a conscience to choose right over wrong, then the major questions (because we are fairly good at teaching facts and skills) become: How do we help develop these attributes in children? What is the source of truth? How does a person decide what is true, what is a lie, what is shaded? On what basis does an adult, a teen, or a child make evaluations of what is good or evil, right or wrong?

As a result of globalization, today's parents, teachers, and learners are being exposed to many different cultures, ideologies, definitions of character virtues, and worldviews as never before. This exposure can be seen as detrimental or as an opportunity. I prefer to see it as an opportunity to develop critical thinking.

Guidelines for Developing Critical Thinking

Remember the questions listed in Chapter Three through which we may evaluate the development of a biblical worldview in ourselves and our children? One of them was, "What is truth?" One way to discern truth is to develop the skill of critical thinking. One way to develop critical thinking in children is through teaching and application of this seven-step approach.

Step 1: Gather the facts through
- Observation (this is the foundation of critical thinking)
- Asking experts (parents, teachers, trusted adults)
- History (familiar or similar experiences)

Questions to ask younger children:
- What do you see or hear?
- What does it look like?
- What does it feel like or smell like?
- Where have you seen it before?
- It is the same or different from what you have seen before?

Questions to ask older children:
- Is the source of the facts reliable?
- Have any of the facts been ignored?
- Have any of the facts been overlooked?
- Are the facts relevant?

Step 2: Order the facts (The skill practiced here is categorization)

Step 3: Make a theory

Step 4: Compare the facts to
- what is known
- what is familiar and then determine if more facts are needed

Step 5: List probabilities

Step 6: Compare probabilities to facts

Step 7: Draw conclusions

Here is an example of a parent-and-child critical thinking interaction using a teachable moment in the home. A parent is in the kitchen slicing a block of white cheese. A preschool age child comes in and asks, "What is that?"

What would be your normal first response? Probably, "It's Mozzarella cheese." When you are teaching critical thinking, however, the better response is not to give answers but create questions or give obvious, incorrect facts to stimulate discussion. Observe the interaction that follows. As you read, take a pencil and label the parent/teacher's use of the seven steps.

Parent/teacher: "This is an apple."

Preschooler: "No, it's not."

Parent/teacher: "How do you know it is not an apple?"

Preschooler: "It's not red."

Parent/teacher: "Oh! Then it must be a tomato."

Preschooler: "No, a tomato is red too."

Parent/teacher: "So it is not an apple and it is not a tomato! It must be water."

Preschooler: "No, it's not water, because it's hard."

Parent/teacher: "It is not an apple or a tomato because it is not red. It is not water because it is solid. What color is it?"

Preschooler: "It's white."

Parent/teacher: "What shape is it?"

Preschooler: "Rectangle."

Parent/teacher: "What other food are you familiar with that is solid, white, and shaped like a rectangle?"

Preschooler: "Tofu."

Parent/teacher: "Good thinking! How can you find out if this is tofu?"

Preschooler: "I can taste it."

Parent/teacher: "Go ahead." (Preschooler tastes.) "What is your conclusion? What have you discovered as you tasted the white, rectangle, solid food?"

Preschooler: "It's cheese!"

Parent/teacher: "Are you sure it doesn't taste like butter?"

Preschooler: "No, it doesn't taste like butter. Besides, butter is yellow. It is cheese. I don't know what kind of cheese. But it is cheese."

Compare your labeling of the use of the seven steps to the following. I have labeled the preschooler's responses as well.

Parent/teacher: "This is an apple."

Preschooler: "No, it's not." *(Gather the facts)*

Parent/teacher: "How do you know it is not an apple?" *(Compare the facts)*

Preschooler: "It's not red." *(Gather the facts)*

Parent/teacher: "Oh! Then it must be a tomato." *(Order the facts)*

Preschooler: "No, a tomato is red too." *(Compare the facts)*

Parent/teacher: "So it is not an apple and it is not a tomato! It must be water." *(Make a theory)*

Preschooler: "No, it's not water, because it's hard." *(Compare the facts)*

Parent/teacher: "It is not an apple or a tomato because it is not red. It is not water because it is hard or solid. What color is it?" *(Compare the facts)*

Preschooler: "It's white." *(Gather the facts)*

Parent/teacher: "What shape is it?" *(Gather the facts)*

Preschooler: "Rectangle." *(Gather the facts)*

Parent/teacher: "What other food are you familiar with that is solid, white, and shaped like a rectangle?" *(Compare the facts)*

Preschooler: "Tofu." *(Draw conclusions)*

Parent/teacher: "Good thinking! How can you find out if this is tofu?" *(Compare probabilities to facts)*

Preschooler: "I can taste it." *(Compare probabilities to facts)*

Parent/teacher: "Go ahead." (Preschooler tastes.) "What is your con clusion? What have you discovered as you tasted the white, rect angle, solid food?" *(Compare probabilities to facts)*

Preschooler: "It's cheese!" *(Draw conclusions)*

Parent/teacher: "Are you sure it doesn't taste like butter?" *(Compare probabilities to facts)*

Preschooler: "No, it doesn't taste like butter. Besides, butter is yellow. It is cheese. I don't know what kind of cheese. But it is cheese." *(Draw conclusions)*

Notice that the steps do not necessarily go one through seven, because if the parent/teacher's or child's statements or theories are incorrect, it is necessary to return to gathering facts or another earlier step. These steps not only help the child reach a conclusion that is true, but they also provide a means for the parent/teacher to know that the child arrived at the correct conclusion.

The use of the seven-step approach in simple, everyday teachable moments lays the foundation for critical thinking in children. Make it fun. Make it a game.

Here is an example of its use in a teachable moment that forti-
fies character virtues. A teacher has asked the children to find a stopping place and move to the story area. Children ignore the repeated
instruction, as do the parent helpers. The use of the steps is noted
for you.

Teacher: "Hold on a moment, guys and gals. We need to take a look
at what is happening in our fourth grade classroom today. Look
at our critical thinking skills chart. What just happened when I
asked us to move to story area?" *(Identify the problem)*
Tracy: "We didn't stop talking."
Geoff: "We kept working and didn't find a stopping place."
Sam: "And the parent helpers kept on talking to each other."
Teacher: "So children continued to talk, they continued to work on
their project, and the parent helpers continued to talk. A character
virtue is missing in this interaction."
Hannah: "Which one is it?" *(Gather the facts)*
Teacher: "Let's think about it. What have we observed?" *(Gather
the facts)*
Simon: "We were talking too much, we didn't find a stopping place,
and the adults didn't stop talking either. Everybody just kept on
talking." *(Gather the facts)*
Teacher: "Have you overlooked anything?"
Kia: "We ignored you; we kept on doing what we wanted to do."
Parent helper: "We kept talking too."
Thomas: "We were not being respectful." *(Make a theory)*
Teacher: "Good thinking! Let's test this theory. Let's compare the
facts."
Nathan: "We kept on talking and working on our project instead
of putting away our materials and gathering for the story." *(Com-
pare the facts)*
Teacher: "What do you think? Could it be responsibility?" *(List
probabilities)*
Thomas: "Responsible people do listen and follow instructions."
(List probabilities)

Amy: "Yes, but it is disrespectful to keep talking when a teacher is giving the instruction." *(List probabilities)*

Teacher: "So which is it—a lack of respect or responsibility?" *(Compare probabilities to facts)*

Tanner: "My conclusion is that it is both. We weren't missing one. We were missing two: respect and responsibility."

Trusted adults in the life of any child have tremendous power. Children will say and do almost anything a mom or dad or favorite teacher tells them. They will make choices based only on the desires of their trusted adult. How much better it is for parents, teachers, and coaches to allow more opportunities to explore, discuss, and compare. The goal needs to be to equip children to discern truth and to make voluntary choices based on truth that comes from testing, doubting, questioning, comparing, and experiencing.

Further Guidelines for Developing Critical Thinking

Besides the seven-step approach, here are further guidelines for helping children develop critical thinking.

1. Do not give answers. Learn to ask questions. This is the number one guideline.

    Where are you in your questioning skills? Are you using

    - open-ended questions?
    - questions that cannot be answered with "yes" or "no"?
    - clarifying questions ("Do you mean...?" "Is this what you are saying?")
    - reframing questions? ("If the apple is not red, what color is it?")

    > Do not give answers. Learn to ask questions. This is the number one guideline.

2. Help children make comparative observations that discern truth and error.

    Example: If a child is playing with another child or interacting with a parent/teacher who demonstrates a different belief system, allow this time to be a platform for discussion and comparison.

3. Guide children to have respect for their teachers and parents and to honor their positions of authority.

One simple way to guide respect is to have the children address their parents and teachers and friends with their respective titles. Mr. Green, Mrs. Greer, or at least Mr. Jim, Miss Shannon. For parents, Mom, Mother, Dad, and Father rather than by the parent's first name.

4. Guide children to question, evaluate, and listen carefully to what is being taught or said by teachers and parents.

Example: A leader sees toys scattered all around and says, "Who is to blame for this mess?" Guide your child to respond to the leader in an appropriate way by saying, "Rather than blaming someone, let's just clean this mess up together."

Here are some practical ideas to help you implement these guidelines.

1. Lay a foundation for children to give them protection from others as they ask questions and articulate different thoughts, attitudes, and ideas. Include the following:
   • rules for talking and discussion in the classroom or home
   • behavior expectations
   • acceptance of their attitudes and ideas

2. Talk about and define constructive choices and destructive choices. Discuss and label choices, and allow logical consequences. Example: "Please choose a place to sit on the circle line (on a chair, at the table). If you are not able to choose, the logical consequence is to sit in the place that I choose for you."

3. Let children know that the Bible is the standard that is measurable and does not change. By measurable, I mean that the Bible is a specified, uniformed, calculated source for measuring truth, attitudes, character response, right and wrong, and much more.

4. Help children learn why they believe what they do. Why do they believe that Jesus is God's Son? How do they know that Jesus died and God brought Him back to life?

5. Guide children to define, practice, apply, and transfer character virtues. They need to know the meaning of the character words you use and how to apply them in their lives.

6. Help children develop a biblical belief system that enables them to discern right and wrong.

7. Help children know how to think about having a personal relationship with God through Jesus. Tell your story of your own personal relationship with Jesus. Be sure to include that they too must make their own decision about their relationship with God.

8. Help children identify what others believe by asking questions. Example: "What do you celebrate at Christmas?"

9. Help children learn how to simply tell children with other belief systems how they can have a personal friendship/relationship with Jesus. Example: "You can ask Jesus to come into your life and be your friend." (I have written a booklet titled "The Greatest Promise" to help children know they can ask Jesus into their life and how to tell others about inviting Jesus into their life. See the Appendix.)

Making the Most of Teachable Moments

Life is filled with teachable moments. I especially want to help parents become aware of teachable moments and understand that parents are the primary teachers of their children. Parents need to make sure that opportunities for growth and development are abundant in the home. I encourage parents to be intentional about including discussion at mealtimes. Mealtimes are prime teaching opportunities when parents can listen to what is going on in their children's lives. They also are a time for parents to develop their skills in asking questions to promote critical thinking.

Many other opportunities exist for parents, teachers, and leaders to use as teachable moments. In everyday conversation, the ideas, words, and phrases that are part of our culture provide teachable moments. These ideas, words, and phrases come from storybooks, cartoon characters, schools, sports, current events/news, music, movies, television programs, and commercials.

A recent commercial depicts an elementary age boy opening a refrigerator, removing a bottle of soda, and shaking it. As he removes the cap, the soda sprays all over the kitchen. The mother yells, "Jimmy, what's wrong with you?" He gives her a frightened look, and she turns to the sink, grabs the water sprayer, and soaks her child. As she does so, she says, "This works a lot better."

The commercial goes on to advertise paper towels. Questions to stimulate conversation as a parent and child watch this commercial might be: "What is a better way for a parent to respond than to yell at a child when there is an accident? What parent would spray water all over the child and the kitchen?" Why would a parent join the child in making a huge mess in the kitchen just because there are paper towels to clean it up?"

Look for opportunities to encourage open discussions. Help children think through ideologies, and help them become aware of others' belief systems. Give equal importance to discussion and conversation as you do to modeling.

Here is an example of a teachable moment for a young child. The child takes a friend's toy without asking him. Instead of saying, "You shouldn't do that," say, "Let's think and talk about this situation together. What happens when you take a friend's toy without asking?"

This is an integrity example of a teachable moment for an older child. The child asks, "Is it ever okay to tell a lie?" Instead of answering the question, say, "Let's think and talk about this question together by taking a piece of notebook paper and a pencil. Write your question at the top of the page. Then draw a line down the middle of the paper to create two columns. Label the column to the left with 'What are the benefits of telling a lie?' Label the column to the right with 'What are the consequences of telling a lie?' After you write some of your ideas, it might be fun to ask other family members and friends to add their ideas. Then we may have a lively discussion."

Critical thinking in children begins with parents, teachers, and other trusted adults who have learned to think critically. Expose yourself to other belief systems. Continue to make intentional strategies to define and articulate your own biblical worldview. Your first task is to increase your skills in thinking and responding critically. One of the results of your effort is for you to become better equipped to help your children think and learn.

NOTES

[1] John Piaget, a French Swiss developmental psychologist, conducted research that has profoundly affected our understanding of child development.

Think on These Things

How is your thinking limited by your perspective? Has it been limited by your environment, by affluence, by lack of justice, or by prejudice?

_____

_____

_____

Describe your perspective on promise keeping.

_____

_____

_____

Practice It!

Children's thinking is limited by their perspective. List a child's perspective on:

Promises _____

_____

_____

Family _____

_____

_____

Children's thinking depends on the quality and quantity of firsthand experiences. Describe a firsthand experience to teach the concept of sharing.

_____

_____

_____

Children's thinking is limited to physical activity. Describe some physical activities to teach the character virtue of perseverance:

_____

_____

CHAPTER EIGHT

Character Language and Communication

"But encourage one another daily."
Hebrews 3:13a

Words have tremendous power. Words are able to create and build relationships, knowledge, attitudes, understanding, and character. The words we use and the way we guide conversation greatly impact character and spiritual formation in children, their families, and communities.

The Importance of Relationships

Children arrive in the world knowing nothing. In a few years, they acquire a vast amount of information. Adult relationships are an important source of help in this learning task.

One of the reasons why relationships are so crucial in character formation and the development of "with-God" life is because children are powerfully influenced by the people they admire. Whatever your role is with the children you serve, you are a teacher. Many of us know or quickly learn that more character and the "with-God" life is "caught" rather than "taught." The modeling and living out of God's character in thought, words, attitudes, and actions in practical daily living is essential to character and spiritual formation in our children.

Opportunities abound for modeling and living out character virtues when traveling. It is a delight to "give away" a virtue through modeling and, in doing so, to encourage others to do the same. Recently while I was waiting in a long line to rebook a canceled flight, I noticed the attitudes and language of fellow travelers being visited with vengeance upon the airline agent. When I reached the counter, I said to the agent, "Would you like to take a deep breath and gather your thoughts for a moment before you tackle my agenda?" The agent gave me a surprised look and replied, "Oh, thank you! Just a swallow of water and a moment to collect my thoughts would really help." I overhead a child behind me remark, "That lady was sure a lot nicer than most everybody else around here."

Guided Conversation Skills

Some people appear to attract children like the proverbial Pied Piper. These people seem to be gifted with a natural talent for building relationships with children that others envy, convinced they cannot attain similar results. Fortunately, there are basic guided conversation skills that can be easily learned and effectively used to build positive relationships with children and model character virtues.

Guided conversation is one of the best methods we can use to communicate meaningfully with children. Guided conversation is an intentional strategy that builds relationships, attitudes, and understanding. Simply defined, *guided conversation* is informal but planned dialogue using nonverbal and verbal communication.

First let's take a look at the nonverbal communication portion of guided conversation. Nonverbal communication takes place through two main channels: facial expressions and body gestures. What examples of facial expressions and body gestures come to your mind?

Guided conversation is informal but planned dialogue using nonverbal and verbal communication.

Here are a few:

Facial expressions—smile, eye contact, frown, surprise, scowl

<u>Body gestures</u>—arms crossed in front of body or down to the side, pointed finger, hand on chin

Can you think of at least one more facial expression and one more body gesture to add to these?

Facial expressions and body gestures communicate openness or distance, acceptance or rejection. For instance, a child may interpret your arms crossed and pressed against your body as a message of withdrawal when in fact you may just be cold. As children arrive in a learning environment or home from school or activities, therefore, it is important for you to turn your body toward them and give eye contact, a smile, and words that describe your positive attitude toward their arrival.

If you are occupied with a task or involved in a conversation with another person when a child approaches you, your nonverbal communication may send a message that you are not ready to be approached by the child or that the person you are talking to is more important than the child. Once again, the unintended nonverbal communication can be corrected by giving eye contact, turning your body toward the child, and offering words that describe your positive attitude toward the child. "Wes, I have looked forward to you being here. Please choose a seat at the table while I finish this task." "Michelle, I am glad you came today. I need to finish my short conversation with this gentleman while you find a place at the table." "Jesse, I am glad your home. I have been looking forward to hearing about your day. I will be off the phone shortly."

Tone of voice also affects communication and is an integral part of guided conversation. Different tones of voice include loud, soft, comforting, and harsh. It's your turn. Think of some others to add to these.

Here is an exercise to help you become aware of the power of nonverbal communication. With a friend, observe each other's nonverbal facial expressions, body gestures, and tone of voice. Then share your observations.

1. Be seated in chairs, facing one another. Ask your friend to observe, identify, and be ready to share with you your nonverbal facial expressions, body gestures, and tone of voice as you talk for one minute about what you like the most about children.

2. After talking for a minute and then listening to your friend's observations of your nonverbal facial expressions, tone of voice, and body gestures, thank your friend. Then ask your friend to talk about what he or she likes the most about children while you observe. Without telling your partner what you are doing, avoid eye contact as he or she talks.

What was your friend's response to your nonverbal communication as you avoided eye contact? What were your feelings and attitudes as you did it? How long were the two of you able to communicate without eye contact?

The responses I hear from the many people who do this exercise in my training seminars include the talker in the second part of the exercise saying, "You're not paying attention to me" or thinking, "What I am saying must be boring." The listener often says, "I felt I was being rude" or, "I could not hear what my partner was saying."

This simple exercise demonstrates the power of nonverbal communication. If the nonverbal communication is not the same as the verbal communication, an incongruent message is given. In this case, the incongruence is due to a verbal, stated desire to listen combined with nonverbal communication (no eye contact) that implies the listener is not really listening.

When an incongruent message is given, the nonverbal will always be heard, and the verbal is often not heard at all. Let the reality of this truth sink into you deeply.

Here is an example: A teacher has had a tense, stressful time prior to meeting with her learners. She greets a child and says, "Hello, I am glad you are here." If her tone of voice or body gestures say, "I am uptight" or "I am rushed," the child will hear the nonverbal tone of voice or see her gesture and interpret it as, "I make my teacher tense. I wonder if she is upset with me. I wonder if she really likes me." A better way for the teacher to communicate, without incongruence, would be to say, "Hello, I am glad I am here. I had a difficult time on my way here. I was rushed, but I'm okay now."

> When an incongruent message is given, the nonverbal will always be heard, and the verbal is often not heard at all.

Guided conversation is the *intentional* combination of facial expressions, body gestures, tone of voice, and actual words. Make a habit of using guided conversation to build positive relationships with children and give definitions to character virtues.

Skills for Building Positive Attitudes

The most effective communication with children of all ages takes place when we combine guided conversation skills with one or more of the following skills for building positive attitudes.

Modeling

Attitudes, emotions, and feelings are communicated by example. Model the attitudes you want to develop in your children. A smile, a hug, and a meeting of the eyes are all nonverbal expressions of the attitude of happiness. Combining your nonverbal expressions with words like "your smile and happy attitude gives me happiness too" enrich these moments by clearly focusing the child's attention on what you are communicating.

Take a moment right now to think about your typical body stances and words as you greet children.

Giving Praise and Encouragement

Children and adults need praise and encouragement far more than they need criticism. Global praise statements are "great," "wonderful," and "good job." Overuse of global praise results in empty praise. To increase the effectiveness of praise and encouragement, be specific. When looking at a child's drawing, you might say, "I like the faces in your picture. I can tell this person is happy and this one is angry. Tell me some more about your drawing."

> Overuse of global praise results in empty praise.

Take a moment to think of some *specific* praise words and times you could use them to encourage a child.

Accepting Emotions and Ideas

Telling (words) and showing (nonverbal) children that you accept them builds positive attitudes. All children need to know that someone cares, understands, and likes them just as they are. Acceptance of ideas does not require agreement or approval. Acceptance is simply letting children know you have heard and understood what they have said.

To communicate acceptance, make what you say to a child simple and true. "I can tell you are bored." "I see your frustration." "That worksheet is confusing." "Leaving your parents is hard."

Take a moment to think of some statements you can use for accepting a child's anger, confusion, tears, or expression of an unrelated idea in the middle of a discussion time.

The following chart is created to motivate you to evaluate how you respond verbally to the children you are serving. Read each statement and then decide your typical response: "most of the time," "occasionally," or "rarely."

Building Positive Attitudes	Most of the time	Occasionally	Rarely
1. I speak to children individually and call them by name.			
2. I verbally express the love I have for teaching.			
3. I name a particular action or accomplishment when praising a child.			
4. I accept a child's negative attitudes and express verbally that I understand.			
5. I acknowledge a positive attitude or action and comment on its relationship to a character virtue.			
6. I accept children's ideas even when they are not entirely correct or are unrelated to a discussion.			
7. I express corrections and boundaries or limitations in positive ways.			

I would like you to practice responding with guided conversation to a few statements a child might make. Remember, the idea is that your nonverbal and verbal communication help build positive attitudes. Write down some conversation ideas to the following situations. Keep in mind your responses in the above chart where you indicated that you "occasionally" or "rarely" employ these skills with your children. Be specific!

1.   You ask a child to draw a picture of his family. The child says, "I can't draw."
2.   You ask a child to share his or her toy. The child says, "No! It's mine."
3.   A child says, "Thank you."

(HINT: First identify what belief, attitude, or action is present in the child's statement. Then determine what verbal or nonverbal communication is needed to model a character virtue, give praise and encouragement, or accept emotions and ideas.)

Compare your responses to these examples:

1.   The child says, "I can't draw." You respond, "It's hard to try something when you're not sure you can do it. Try making a circle. Good. Now put a small rectangle with the short side of the rectangle under the circle. Then put short lines coming out from the right and the left sides of the rectangle. How does what you are making begin to look like a head, neck, and arms? Trying something new tells me you are a person of courage and perseverance."

    The I can't attitude is built on fear of failure. Children need the freedom to try and fail without loss of acceptance or status. Help children understand that failure is part of learning.

2.   The child says, "No! It's mine." You respond, "Here is a toy that is mine. You may share my toy with your friend. You are becoming a person who likes to share."

    Young children have a difficult time sharing an object that is theirs. By offering a toy that is not their own, you enable the attitude change and the opportunity to label the child as one who shares.

3. A child says, "Thank you." You respond, "You're welcome! Being thanked by you lets me know you are becoming a grateful person."

Children need specific evaluation of character actions and attitudes. They also need praise and encouragement when they show positive character qualities.

Skills for Building Understanding and Developing Character Language

I have discovered six effective skills for helping children understand and begin to use character language. As you read through these, please notice the specific words used, which are examples of character language.

Labeling

To label means to give a child a familiar or concrete name for a character virtue.

Example: "Sharing is an act of compassion."
Example: "Living in community with our parents, family, teachers, and friends gives the opportunity to share, care, and become people of compassion."
Parents, teachers, and coaches who are aware that children need words to build understanding do a great deal of labeling, naturally and easily, in a wide variety of experiences.

Describing

Children need to hear simple accounts of what is going on around them.

Example: "Sharon is having a problem with her drawing. What can you do to help her?"

Example: "We live our lives with God. He is with us all the time, in every place, helping us think and say the right things and be kind and forgiving to each other."

Describing helps children be aware of others' needs and builds compassion and awareness of a "with-God life."

Explaining

Explaining involves giving a child reasons and definitions.

Example: "Tommy, sharing your pencil with Sharon is a kind and compassionate thing to do. Sharon needs that pencil to finish her drawing. Caring that your friend does not have a pencil is an act of compassion."

Stimulating

You build a child's understanding by stimulating curiosity with open-ended questions. Open-ended questions call for a child to share his or her attitudes, ideas, and opinions, not just memorized answers.

Example: "What did you like best about being kind and compassionate when you shared your pencil with Sharon? Why?"

Giving Directions

Keep your directions simple, brief, and clear. Give them one at a time.

Example: "Please choose crayons or felt pens. Now, please draw a picture of your family. Thank you for following the directions. Responsible people follow directions, and you are becoming a responsible person."

Enabling

This skill helps children build understanding by discovering some information on their own. Their interest and confidence grow as they are able to succeed independently.

Example: Before Tommy gave his pencil to Sharon, his teacher said, "Sharon is having a problem with her drawing. What could you do to help her?" Tommy solved the problem by giving Sharon a pencil.

The teacher's question enabled Tommy to practice an act of compassion and to succeed.

All these skills are important, but I want to emphasize the skill of describing. Describing helps with the common problem many teachers and parents experience with unacceptable language they hear when interacting with children. Some words and phrases that children use to express anger and frustration are unacceptable. Profanity is one. Insults are another.

Unacceptable words do not describe emotions or attitudes. Since these words and phrases are not accurate, they result in misunderstandings and wounded people. An example is the phrase, "That is a stupid thing to say!"

Words or phrases that are not acceptable need to be replaced with ones that are. Describe the unacceptable words with learners, and guide them to replace unacceptable words or phrases with appropriate ones. Instead of saying, "That's a stupid thing to say!" you could say, "I don't agree with what you just said." This response helps children learn to use "I" statements.

Children also need to be given acceptable words or phrases that describe their emotions and attitudes, "I am sad." "I am angry." "I am frustrated." We need to take our children to the place where they describe a hurt finger with, "Oh, I banged my finger, and it really hurts!" instead of an unacceptable word or phrase. The goal is to fill the air with meaningful language.

Techniques to Enhance Guided Conversation

In my years of serving children and teaching others who serve children, I have had many firsthand experiences using guided conversation techniques that work as well as ones that do not work. Here is my "best techniques" list.

1. Desire to listen and discover what children think. This is essential. Expect to learn from them. Ask for clarification. Their ideas may be different from yours, and their experi-

> Desire to listen and discover what children think. Expect to learn from them.

ences may differ from those you are suggesting. For instance, you may think that a story about a boy named Carlos is sending a certain message about lies. By asking the question, "Please tell me what you think about Carlos telling a lie?" you discover what the children really understand or believe.

2. Ask one question at a time. Children have difficulty with complex sentences or a series of questions. Say, "Is it ever okay to tell a lie?" instead of "Is it ever okay to tell a lie, and do you have an example of a time when you told a lie that you think is okay?"

3. Allow time for children to think. Ask, "What is this Bible verse helping you do?" and then wait for an answer. Count to ten before you assume a child is not able to answer.

4. Reveal the source of your answers to a child's question. "I know this is true because it is in God's book the Bible. It's in the New Testament in the book called John."

5. Clarify the difference between fact and opinion. Brady comments that all the children in the class like to draw. His teacher says, "Let's see if that is a fact or your opinion. All those who like to draw, raise a hand." Six raise a hand and four do not. The teacher then says, "Brady, was your comment a fact or an opinion?"

6. Clarify the difference between questions and statements. "It takes perseverance to do my homework?" says Wai Hing. The teacher responds, "Is your remark a question or a statement? If it is a question, you are letting me know that you want to know more about perseverance. If it is a statement, the answer is, it does take a lot of perseverance to do homework."

7. Check the clarity of your question, and be willing to rephrase a follow-up question. When you ask, "What did Tommy do?" a child may respond, "I don't know what you mean." If you respond, "Well, what did Tommy do?" then the child knows no more than he or she did at the beginning of the conversation. Instead, rephrase the question. "What did Tommy do when Sharon did not have a pencil?"

8. Use a visual to help a child's understanding of your question. A picture can be used to illustrate your question.

9. Thank learners for sharing their thoughts and answers. "Good thinking, John. Thank you for your thought and respectful answer."

10. Allow children to choose not to answer. "It is okay to think about this. Let me know if you need more information in order to participate."

Avoid these four types of questions.

1. *Questions that create Yes/No responses,* which limit a child's thinking and restrict further conversation or require another question.

2. *Ambiguous questions,* which may confuse the child about what is expected.

3. *Spoon-feeding questions,* which present information so completely that a child is left with no room for independent thought.

4. *Multiple factor questions,* which confuse a child with too much to think of at one time.

The most effective way to build character is through contact with people who reflect God's character in thoughts, attitudes, words, and actions. Building positive relationships with children is, therefore, an essential and highly rewarding task. Guiding children's character and spiritual formation includes the use of guided conversation skills, skills for building positive attitudes, and understanding the development of character language. The essence of character language is so vital. It is not just words. It is words plus the nonverbal, the tone of voice, and the building of positive attitudes and understanding.

> The most effective way to build character is through contact with people who reflect God's character in thoughts, attitudes, words, and actions.

Think on These Things

A child can follow an example much easier than an exhortation. Think back to some of your childhood experiences with parents or teachers.

- Their names and favorite sayings
- What you liked best and least about them
- The nickname you and your siblings or classmates had for them
- What you looked forward to doing at home or in their classroom
- The gifts your gave them on special days
- How they dealt with unacceptable behavior
- The language they used to give you a sense of worth and belonging

Practice It!

Look again at the four types of questions to avoid. Rephrase the following questions. All questions in each set share a similar problem.

Type 1: *Yes/No questions*, which limit a child's thinking and restrict further conversation or require another question.

- Was Angelina angry at her mother?

  _____

- Did she ask for forgiveness?

  _____

- Can you think of a reason Angelina was so angry?

  _____

Type 2: *Ambiguous questions,* which may confuse the child about what is expected.

- How about Carlos?

  _____

- How long do you think Carlos was going to lie to his parents?

  _____

- Tell me about squash plants.

  _____

Type 3: *Spoon-feeding questions* in which information is presented so completely that the child is left no room for independent thought.

- So we can say David helped his father, can't we?

  _____

- Wouldn't you sing to your sheep to comfort them if you were a shepherd?

  _____

- If David had refused to watch his father's sheep, he wouldn't be doing what his father asked, would he?

  _____

  _____

Type 4: *Multiple factor questions* that confuse the child with too much to think of at one time.

- What is a shepherd, and can you tell me why shepherds sing to their sheep?

  _____

- What do you think David did while he was with his sheep, and do you think he became lonely?

  _____

CHAPTER NINE

Using Stories and Activities to Develop Character

"Jesus used stories to tell all these things to the people. He always used stories to teach people."
Matthew 13:34 (ICB)

"He {Jesus} taught by using stories, many stories."
Mark 4:2 (MSG)

Tell me a story! How often do you hear this plea from a child? What goes through you mind when you hear it? How do you respond?

The Power of Stories

Children are able to relate easily to people in stories. They recognize the elements of stories with which they are already familiar. They remember the people's virtues. Most important, as they hear or read about the people's story beliefs, behaviors, attitudes, actions, character, and conduct, children begin to transfer the people's virtues into their own lives. In doing so, the inward transformation process of becoming people who reflect God's character is taking place.

Jesus models storytelling in his teachings. He is the proverbial storyteller. He uses stories to illustrate and apply truths about His Father God, the kingdom of God, and the everyday, walk-around "with-God life."

Storytelling is an intentional strategy that most people enjoy. Storytelling skills improve through practice. Most important, however, the use of stories is one of the most effective ways to develop character and conscience in children. Here is a responsibility story.

I FORGOT

It was one of those days you read about in stories: bright blue sky and sunshine. Gabrielle jumped from behind a bush and made Mark giggle. She laughed, too, and spun around and around. She didn't mind watching three-year-old Mark sometimes. Mom was fixing lunch and it was a great day to be outside. She sat down on the grass and watched her little brother on his tricycle.

"Come on in, you two. Lunch is ready," called Mom from the kitchen window.

Gabrielle swung Mark up and over the trike, set him down, and challenged, "I'll race you to the door!"

Mark took off on his little legs, and Gabrielle pretended to try to catch him. She let him reach the door first, and he chanted, "I won, I won!"

"Honey, Mark's tricycle is on the driveway. Please go out and put it on the porch," said Gabrielle's mom as she put lunch on the table.

"I will, Mom, right after I eat. I'm starved!"

"Okay, but don't forget," answered Mom patiently.

"I won't forget." Gabrielle assured her, a little aggravated that her mother thought she might not remember.

After lunch Mark was sent off for a nap while Gabrielle helped clear the table. "Don't forget to put that trike on the porch," reminded Mom.

"I didn't forget, Mom. I'm going to do it right now," answered Gabrielle, with an edge to her voice. "Why does Mom have to remind me?" she thought. "I'm not going to forget."

As Gabrielle went out the door, she saw Tracy and Becky coming toward her. "Hi!" she called as she ran to meet them. "What are you two planning?"

"We're going over to Landers field," said Becky. "Tracy's mom said there are millions of wildflowers blooming. You want to come? Afterward we're going to play ball with Shauna and Rose. Come on."

"It'll be more fun if you come," chimed in Tracy.

"Mom," Gabrielle called, seeing her mother at the window. "Can I go with Becky and Tracy?"

"Okay. But be back before dark."

As the girls ran off to play, and while Mark peacefully slept, a small tricycle sat all alone in the middle of the driveway.

That Saturday afternoon went by all too fast. Gabrielle was tired but happy as she headed home. Her arms were full of half-wilted wildflowers picked from Landers field earlier in the day. She hoped the flowers would revive when she put them in water.

As Gabrielle neared her house, she noticed the driveway was empty. Then it hit her! She had forgotten the tricycle. She had forgotten to put it on the porch. But where was it? Maybe her mother had moved it. She looked on the porch. There was no tricycle there. She looked in the yard. No tricycle.

Maybe if she said nothing, Gabrielle thought, the whole thing would be forgotten, just as she had forgotten the trike. She went into the house as quietly as she could, hoping to slip in without being noticed.

Mark was in the living room playing with his toy truck. He looked up at her, and Gabrielle was surprised to see he had been crying. "A truck ran over my tricycle," he told her solemnly. "It's all broken and won't go."

Before Gabrielle could react, her mother came into the room. Gabrielle could see she was not very happy. "Even though I reminded you, you forgot! The driver felt terrible. Mark is so sad. I am disappointed. What are your attitudes and reactions?"

"Oh, Mom," began Gabrielle, "I don't know what to say. You told me not to forget. You did remind me, and I was mad. I had a big attitude attack. I was sure I wouldn't forget. I was wrong. Oh Markie, I am so sorry your tricycle is broken."

Well, what has happened, happened," answered Mom. "But now, what can be done? Let's think about what's happened. Being responsible is both an individual and a family choice."

Gabrielle went to her room, still clutching the wildflowers in her arms. They didn't seem too important now. Mother was correct. Gabrielle wondered, "How can I make more responsible choices?"

"Dear God," Gabrielle prayed, "please help me understand what I can do to correct this mistake and make it better for Mark. Please help me become more responsible."

Gabrielle lifted her big dictionary off the shelf. "I'm going to find out just what responsible means," she whispered to herself. She looked up the word responsible. The dictionary said it meant "trustworthy, reliable, accountable, dependable, capable, competent."

She went to the Internet and found an article that said, "Responsibility means personal and individual acceptance that every person is accountable for his or her behavior, including thoughts, choices, decisions, speech, and actions."

Gabrielle admitted to herself that her thoughts and choices had resulted in the destruction of her brother's tricycle and in his sense of loss and sadness. She began to make a plan to correct her mistake.

"Mom," Gabrielle said the next day when they all returned from church. "I know that what happened yesterday was my mistake. You asked me to do something, and I forgot. I want you to know that beginning today; I am asking God to help me become a reliable person. I want to become trustworthy."

Gabrielle's mom was grateful. Gabrielle was choosing to allow her mistake to teach her how to become responsible.

Gabrielle continued, "Last night I wrote an apology to the truck driver. I don't know how to send it to him. Would you send it for me, Mom?"

"Of course, Gabrielle. I'm really proud of your attitude."

Then Gabrielle turned to Mark, who didn't seem interested in all this talk. He was much more interested in having lunch at the earliest possible moment. "Markie," Gabrielle began, "it was wrong of me to leave your tricycle in the driveway where the truck ran over it. Dad and I talked about it last might, and Daddy thinks it can be fixed if we buy a new wheel." Gabrielle saw Dad wink at her as she said that part.

"So, I'm going to clean out the garage and weed the area out back to earn the money to buy a new wheel for your trike. Dad's going to fix it so it will be almost as good as new."

Mark's eyes widened with delight. "Thank you, Gabrielle, for fixing your forgetfulness!"

"Well," Mom began. "I think this young lady is becoming a responsible person."

Gabrielle beamed. Yesterday she too had felt terrible, sad, and disappointed, just like the truck driver, Mark, and Mom. Today she knew she had made the best choices. Being responsible wasn't so bad after all. In fact, it was downright fun!'

How comfortable are you at telling stories? Following are guidelines to help you become more comfortable and a more effective storyteller.

General Storytelling Guidelines

Developing your storytelling skills will not only make you a better storyteller, but it will also increase your learners' involvement and retention.

- <u>Know the story well</u>. Be able to tell the story rather than read it. Telling the story in your own words adds interest and allows you to vary your tone of voice, make eye contact, and use motions.
- <u>Keep the story simple</u>. Use words that your children understand, and avoid metaphors and symbolism. Keep your sentences brief and direct. Focus on one major point.
- <u>Set the scene</u>. Tell something about where and when the story occurs. For example, you might say that the Old

Testament story of Joseph occurs in a faraway country, a long time ago. There were no TVs, telephones, or cars then. When applicable, choose a picture to illustrate the where and when.

- <u>Vary your voice</u>. Change your volume, tone, and rate of speech to fit the story line.
- <u>Be creative in the telling</u>. Think outside the box. For example, if you are telling the story of Jesus calming the storm, create sound effects to accompany it. Drive through a car wash, record the sound of the water hitting on the car, and then play the recording as you tell the story.
- <u>Use dialogue</u>. Put words in the characters' mouths, creating memorable scenes to avoid long, descriptive monologue.
- <u>Vary the presentation</u>. Alternate storytelling techniques so your children expect something interesting and different when you announce that it is story time.

One morning Shannon, a volunteer teacher in Sunday school, approached her lead teacher and said, "I would like to tell the Bible story." "I'm happy to hear you are interested," replied the teacher. "Here are some pictures, and there are story helps in the curriculum." For the next few Sundays, Shannon did the Bible story time by reading the story that was printed on the back of the picture. The receptiveness of reading the story with pictures every Bible story time decreased the effectiveness of her storytelling.

With a little encouragement from the lead teacher, Shannon began to vary her presentation by telling the story while a child held the picture. Then she added sound effects and varied her tone of voice. Then one morning she asked the question, "How was David being a responsible person when he took food to his brothers?" Sam raised his hand and said, "I know, he took the responsibility to go by himself to bring the food to his brothers. Miss Shannon, I really like it when you let us answer questions!"

Storytelling Techniques

There are many techniques you can use to enhance your storytelling. Because we live in a visual image culture and children think concretely, the following techniques help children focus, connect with, and enjoy a story as they become part of the experience. You may be familiar with several of these ideas, but I hope you are inspired to increase your repertoire.

- <u>Tell the story with pictures</u>. Flannel graph and large pictures with simple art are more effective with young children. Older children enjoy more detailed pictures and artwork.
- <u>Illustrate the story with video/DVD clips</u>. I used *Finding Nemo* to illustrate a forgiveness story by changing the theme line "just keep swimming" to "just keep forgiving." *The Story of Jesus for Children* video/DVD (see the Appendix) has numerous clips of various New Testament stories.
- <u>Use simple drama. Act out the story yourself</u> or invite other adults to act out various parts. As the storyteller, dress in costume. Narrate the story as the Bible character. Dress as Moses in a robe with staff and sandals to tell the story of the burning bush.
- <u>Include children in the drama</u>. Children also enjoy acting out stories. Help them identify characters needed and choose a part. Children may want to create or choose costumes if you have them. Retell the story, prompting children with appropriate words and actions.
- <u>Use animals as narrators</u>. Give an animal a voice, and tell the story from the animal's point of view. Become one of the animals on Noah's ark, be the big fish that swallows Jonah, or be the donkey or other animal in the stable when Jesus was born.
- <u>Allow puppets to tell the story</u>. Use puppets to model character virtues. I have created nine puppets, named each one with a character virtue, and created a personality for each one that reflects the virtue: Carrie Compassion, Felicia Forgiveness, Izzy Integrity, Respectful Ramie, Richie Responsibility, Ignacio

Initiative, Corrie and Cooper Cooperation (they are twins), and Pete Perseverance.

- <u>Have children make and use puppets</u>. You can also plan for children to use hand puppets that they make. For the story of Daniel in the lions' den, have younger children make lion puppets before the storytelling. Instruct them to hold the puppet up each time they hear the word *lion*.

- <u>Involve children before you tell the story</u>. Give them a listening assignment. For the Old Testament Bible story of Joseph and his brothers in Egypt, you might say something like this: "Joseph had a choice to make. He could choose to forgive or not to forgive his brothers for something they did that was very wrong. Listen and be ready to tell what choice Joseph made."

- <u>Involve the children as you tell the story</u>. Encourage children to hold pictures for all to see at appropriate times in the story. Invite them to place and move figures on flannel as the story develops. Children eagerly respond to helping place and move figures as directed by the storyteller during the story. You can even invite them to tell the part of the story that they know. This technique also gives you the opportunity to correct previous misunderstandings.

- <u>Use motions, movements</u>, and sound effects. Insert gestures, exaggerated facial expressions, and movements to illustrate words and actions as the story is told. Or lead the children in actions, movements, and sound effects. For example, children may be asked to march when the characters in the story march, such as in the story of Joshua at Jericho.

The use of motion, movement, and sound effects is an especially good technique for increasing interest and retention. The following is a portion of a compassion story, "Four Friends Choose to Help." It gives a good example of using motion and movement. As you read, notice that this story already contains directions for voice inflections and movements. Most stories will not have these included, but many stories lend themselves to this storytelling technique.

People were coming from every town in Galilee and from all over the countryside of Judea! Moms and dads, grandmas and grandpas, and children walked together singing and telling stories as they found their way to the house where Jesus was teaching.

Besides telling the people about God, Jesus was making sick people well. Jesus would touch them with his hand. **(Touch your hand to your leg.)** When he did, people who were not able to walk would be able to walk and run and jump. Jesus would touch people who had never been able to see, **(Touch your hands near your eyes.)** and they would shout, "I can see, I can see."

Now at the same time these wonderful things were taking place, there was a man who lived in the nearby town of Capernaum. He could not move his arms or his legs. He watched the children and the moms and dads walking past him. **(Move your head from right to left to demonstrate watching people pass by. Keep your arms and legs from moving to demonstrate that they are paralyzed.)** "Oh," he thought, "what would it be like if I were able to jump up and stand on my own two feet? What would it be like to run barefoot across a field of soft, green grass?"

Read the next story, "Run Away," which is a story about forgiveness. As you read, put in your own motions and movements. Choose the age group for your storytelling, and create age-appropriate motions, movements, and sound effects for this story segment.

The son decided to change his attitude and go home. He said to himself, "I will go back to my father. I will say to him, 'Father, I have not obeyed God, and I have thought and said and done wrong things to you. I don't deserve to be your son. Please, will you let me work as your servant?'"

The son went back to his own country and home. He did not know that his father had been watching for him and hoping he would come home. But the father had! All of a sudden, the father saw his son coming from a long way off!

The father ran quickly to meet his son, and hugged and kissed him! He looked at his son and felt great compassion for him. He saw that his son had lost everything and was dirty from feeding pigs and traveling. The son said, "Father, I have thought, said, and done many wrong things to you. I have not pleased God. I am not good enough to be your son. I am sorry."

But the father was so excited to see his son again that he said to his servants, "Hurry! Let's have a party! My son has returned. He is alive!" They all celebrated the son's return. The father had forgiven the son even before he had come home. The son was very thankful that his father chose to forgive him.

Storytelling techniques may be combined in various ways to create greater impact. Think now about involving children in the telling of the "Run Away" story. Which of the above techniques would you combine to move from just telling the story to more actively involve the children in the story as it is being told?

The Power of Activities

The words *active* and *children* go together. Design activities to meet the need of children being active. Intentionally designed activities create opportunities for continued exploration, practice, and application of a particular character virtue and its truth. Activities help children put the truth of the virtue into practice. They make possible the practice needed to direct the thinking, language, and choosing of attitudes, actions, and responses in children's everyday lives.

Activities need to be designed to actively involve children's intellect as well as have physical and social aspects. They need to allow the use of all five senses, provide the opportunity to make choices, and offer a way for children to make a life application, which begins the transform and transfer experience.

Guidelines for Activities

The guidelines that follow have proven to be very successful in creating effective character-building activities.

- Vary the types of activities. Choose according to the children's needs and interests.
- Involve adults in activities by sitting at a table or work area and using guided conversation to interact with children.
- Offer a choice of activities. Children are more likely to enjoy learning when they can make choices and be successful in what they are doing. The number of choices depends upon variables such as ages of the learners, motivation, social skills, and reading ability.
- Maintain a ratio of one adult to every six to eight learners to maximize the effectiveness of the activity.
- Plan the number of and the movement between activities. Limit the number of different activities at one time to the number of adults available. For example, if you have two leaders, you might plan, within the same room, an art activity for one leader to guide in one learning area and a game for another adult to guide in another learning area. As children complete one activity, guide them to move to the other activity.
- Limit the number of children at an activity by limiting the number of places to sit. If the activity area is full, the leader guides the latest arriving learners to another activity. Older children may move independently from one activity to another as they complete each activity.

Types of Activities

Curriculum guides often have graphic designs or icons to help leaders quickly identify types of activities. Vary the type of activity to enhance interest and increase new experiences. Any activity can become a tool for character practice and application by intentional focus on a character virtue.

The following six activity types lend themselves well to character building:

- Art: Art offers a wide range of possibilities for creative expression and relaxed opportunities to express ideas and attitudes. Activities include drawing,

TYPES OF ACTIVITIES

Art

Drama

Games and Puzzles

Music

Oral/Written Communication

Science

painting, coloring, clay or play dough, puppet construction, and much more.

- Drama: Drama includes role play, reenacting stories, and the use of puppets.

- Games and Puzzles: Games may be played indoors or outdoors. Puzzles also reinforce the concept of a lesson.

- Music, Rhymes, and Finger Plays: Each of these can be used to reinforce spiritual truths and character virtues. It is relatively easy to create new "character verses" to familiar songs, rhymes, or finger plays.

- Oral and Written Communication: Oral and written communication can be used for discussing the application of a character virtue, sequencing events in a story, writing or dictating a different end to a story, and writing or drawing cards of thanks or sympathy.

- Science: Science offers children the opportunity to discover truths about their world and to further develop critical thinking skills. Activities might include a tasting experiment to discern what a particular food item is. Combine materials together in a way to demonstrate a physical reaction or minor explosion to illustrate a reaction that occurs when people combine envy and jealously, which explode into attitudes of anger and revenge.

I have included here some sample activities from materials my Character Choice ministry team has written for teaching and training. The first is an art activity: "Draw A Mural" from a cooperation session, "Four Friends." Children cooperate to draw a mural to show the beginning, middle, and end of the story "Four Friends Choose to Help."

The second is a science activity: "Touch, Taste, Hear, Smell, and See" from an integrity session, "Daniel Chooses to Pray." In this activity, there are five experiments to help the practice of the family virtue of discernment.

The third is a drama activity: "Act It Out!" from a forgiveness session, "Run Away." In this activity, children act out the story of the boy who ran away from home.

Activity One: Cooperation

DRAW A MURAL
An Art Activity

 Note to Leader: Children cooperate to draw a mural to show the beginning, middle, and end of the story, *Four Friends Choose to Help.* You may choose to use the completed mural for a bulletin board for the Cooperation Module.

Divide children into three groups with one leader each or work with one group of children at a time:
- The Beginning: Four Friends Carry a Man to Jesus
- The Middle: Four Friends Make a Hole in the Roof
- The End: Jesus Heals the Man

When the mural sections are completed, have the children help determine which order the sections should be hung on the bulletin board or wall. Review the story again by having the children tell about the part they drew.

 Preparation/Materials Needed: Tape three sections of butcher paper on the floor or on a table. Place crayons/markers on floor or table.

 Guided Conversation:

We are going to show and tell the story we listened to by creating a mural. A mural is a series of pictures drawn on a long piece of fabric or paper. We are going to use paper.

First, let's remember what happened in the story, *Four Friends Choose to Help.* What did the four friends do first? (decided to take their friend to Jesus, figured out a way to cooperate to take him to Jesus) **Then what did they do?** made a hole in the roof) **What did Jesus say and do?** (Jesus said, "Stand up and walk." Jesus healed the man.)

We have three pieces of butcher paper for each part of the story, one for the beginning of the story, one for the middle of the story, and one for the end of the story. We need at least one person and no more than _____ (whatever number you need to divide your group of children into) **to draw on each section.**

Think about which part of the story you would like to help draw. Think of your first choice and what would be your second choice. You may need to do your second choice. Ready? Who would like to draw the beginning of the story? (allow children to choose, guiding them to make their second choice if needed) **Who would like the middle of the story? Who would like to draw the end of the story?**

When the mural is finished, we will have practiced working together to create a drawing that tells our story. We are becoming cooperative people.

O- - -lult is in your group to guide you as you cooperate to decide what to place in your part of the mural. (Each leader guides the children to plan what each one will draw. Distribute crayons/markers. Encourage children to include details and to sign their names to the part they draw. Assist as needed sharing crayons, markers and clean up.)[20]

Activity Two: Integrity (family virtue: discernment)

ACTIVITIES
to
Apply-Practice-Transform-Transfer
Integrity
Touch, Taste, Hear, Smell, and See

Preparation/Materials Needed:

Prepare five experiment areas:

    #1 Touch: sandpaper, fuzzy material

    #2 Taste: lemon slices, sugar

    #3 Hear: guitar, drum

    #4 Smell: vinegar, vanilla

    #5 See: one red, one yellow, and one blue object (or what is available)

Cover objects in each area so children are not able to view, taste, smell, or touch before you begin. Gather blindfolds for each group.

Leader: In this activity, we have five experiments to help us practice discernment. Look with me at the word sign Izzy gave us. Read and repeat the word with me: discernment. Discernment means to perceive or recognize clearly. One of the ways we can recognize something clearly is to use our five senses to touch, taste, hear, smell, and see.

For the first four experiments, you have the fun opportunity to wear a blindfold so you can use your senses to touch, taste, hear, and smell. For the fifth experiment, you need to take off your blindfold so you can use your sense of sight.

(Divide your children into as many groups as you have adults. Rotate each group through the five areas. Loosely tie the blindfold on the child before beginning the experiment. Guide child as needed. Before leaving each area, replace the child's blindfold.)

Experiment 1—Touch

Leader: You have been led to the "touch area." Please take turns and feel the objects in front of you. You may wish to rub your fingers over the object. Does the object feel rough or smooth? (allow children to feel) **How do you know it is rough?** (it scratches my finger) **What else can you clearly recognize?** (allow children's responses) **You have used your sense of touch to perceive what is true about these objects. What other sense could you use to clearly recognize these objects? Correct... your eyes, or sight. Please take off your blindfolds. Look with your eyes at the two pieces you touched. You could not tell with your eyes which was rough or smooth. With both your sight and your touch, you were able to clearly recognize or discern these objects. What are they?** (allow responses)

Experiment 2—Taste
Leader: **You have been led to the "taste area." Please take turns and taste the food in front of you. Which tastes sour or bitter? Which food is sweet?** (allow children to taste and respond) **What do you think the sour or bitter food is? What do you think the sweet food is? What other sense could you use to clearly recognize these foods? Please take off your blindfolds. You could guess what the foods were by tasting them, but to clearly recognize or truthfully discern the food you need to taste and see. What do you discern these foods to be?** (allow responses)

Experiment 3—Hear
Leader: **You have been led to the "hearing area." Please be silent and listen to two different instruments. Please listen carefully to discern which sound is made by beating and which sound is made by strumming.** (beat drum, strum guitar) **What is the name of the instrument whose sound was made by beating? What is the name of the instrument whose sound was made by strumming? How can you be sure? Please remove your blindfolds and look at the two instruments. Because you listened carefully with your ears, you were able to tell which instrument was beaten and which instrument was strummed. To clearly recognize or truthfully discern the sounds and the names of the instruments, you needed to hear and see.**

Experiment 4—Smell
Leader: **Now you have been led to the "smell area." Please be very still as you smell two different smells.** (hold small jars of vinegar and vanilla so that the child can smell) **What do you smell? Which smell is a pleasant smell? How would you describe the other smell? What do you think you have smelled? How can you be sure? What other sense could you use to clearly recognize these liquids?** (taste or sight) **Please remove your blindfolds. You could guess what the liquids were by smelling them; but to clearly recognize or truthfully discern the type of liquid, you need to smell and see it.**

Experiment 5—See
Leader: **You have walked to the "seeing area." The items on this table are covered. As I** re~~~~ the cover from each item silently look at the item. Look carefully to discern what it is. . .....e raise your hand and wait for your name to be called when you clearly recognize the color and the name of the item.** (allow children to respond) **Thank you for thinking carefully. By using your sight and thinking skills, you were able to recognize and truthfully discern the color and name of each item.**[21]

Activity Three: Forgiveness

ACT IT OUT

 Preparation/Materials Needed: Review the skit script. Make copies of the script for the children to read. Gather simple props such as a suitcase, coat and hat, and other clothing.

Leader: In this activity, we are going to act out the story about the boy who ran away from home. In God's book, the Bible, Jesus tells this story. I will need someone to pretend to be Jesus and help me narrate, or tell the story. We also will need a father, two sons, and a pig farmer, perhaps a pig or two, and, of course, an audience.

(Print a chart with the parts needed as shown below. Guide the children to choose parts, write their names next to their choice, and put on simple costumes. Set up simple props if available. If time allows, repeat the play so that everyone may have a chance to have a speaking part. Children may play more than one part, if needed.)

Our characters are:
      Father played by _____
      Older son played by _____
      Younger son played by _____
      Pig farmer played by _____
      Jesus, our narrator, played by _____
      And of course our wonderful audience played by you.
      (point to audience, clap)
      (Give a copy of the script to each child guiding them to find their lines.)

Leader: Okay. When you are ready to act out your part, raise your hand. This side of the room is the house, and the other side of the room is the exciting place that is far away from home.

Leader: The name of our play is "The Son Who Ran Away." The story begins with the father and his two sons working with each other in the field by their house. (allow time for the children to pretend to work)

Father: "I am so glad I have two sons."

Older son: "We have a good life."

Younger son: "I am not happy here. I would love to go live in a more exciting place."

Narrator, Jesus: "One day the young son decided to leave his home so he went to talk to his dad."

Younger son: "Dad, I know that part of your land is mine. I want you to pay me for my share now."

Father: "I am surprised! But okay, Son. Here is the money for your part of the land."

Younger son: "Thank you, Dad."

Narrator, Jesus: "The son took it all and went far away. (young son walks to the other end of the room) At first, he was happy. (young son acts happy) He did whatever he wanted, and he went wherever he wanted to go." (young son moves around happily)

Younger son: "I can go anywhere, do anything, and buy anything. I am happy!"

Narrator, Jesus: "Before long, the young son had a problem."

Younger son: "I am out of money. I can't even buy food. I have to get a job. (young son moves toward pig farmer) Do you have a job for me? I need money to buy food."

Pig farmer: "You can work for me and feed the pigs."

Younger son: (sadly) "Thank you." (sadly and quietly) "I wish I could go home. I am so hungry that I want to eat what these pigs are eating! I need to go home. I chose to think, say, and do some wrong things. I need to ask my father for forgiveness."
(younger son slowly walks toward home)

Narrator, Jesus: "His father saw him coming. He felt compassion for his son." (father holds his hands over his eyes and pretends to look down the road, then runs to meet and hug the young son as he gets closer to the house)

Younger son: "Dad, please forgive me for all the wrong things I have thought, said, and done. I do not deserve to be your son. Will you hire me to be your servant?"

Fa'   "Son, you are forgiven. I am so happy! My son went away, but now he has come home. Let's have a party to celebrate!"
(everyone jumps for joy and hugs each other)

Narrator, Jesus: "The end."[22]

My hope is that this chapter has illustrated the importance of using stories and activities to create ways to communicate, practice, and apply character virtues. Stories and activities bring concrete situations and experiences to character development and make it enjoyable, fun, and practical to a child's daily living.

NOTES

[19] Vernie Schorr, *Building Character* (Character Choice, Inc., 2001), Unit Six, Lesson 23.

[20] Vernie Schorr, *Building Character* (Character Choice, Inc., 2004), Module 7 Cooperation Session 31.

[21] Vernie Schorr, *Building Character* (Character Choice, Inc., 2004), Module 3 Integrity Session 12 Pre-K.

[22] Vernie Schorr, *Building Character* (Character Choice, Inc., 2006), Module 2 Forgiveness Session 6 Pre-K.

Think on These Things

Think of a story you read in the past six months that you would label "powerful." Write down a few ideas about this story that made your remember it and label it powerful.

_____

_____

Practice It!

List at least three of your favorite children's stories. Jot down one reason why each one is one of your favorites.

_____

_____

Choose one of the three favorite stories, decide what character virtue you could teach using it, and decide what story technique you would like to use to tell the story. Record your choices here.

_____

_____

Choose and circle one activity type you would like to use to help your children practice the virtue of the story: art, drama, games and puzzles, music, oral/written communication, or science. If you have a specific idea for the activity, record it here.

_____

_____

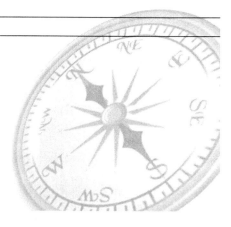

CHAPTER TEN

Using Music Experiences

*"Let the teaching of Christ live in you richly. Use all wisdom to teach
and strengthen each other. Sing psalms, hymns and spiritual songs
with thankfulness in your hearts to God."*
Colossians 3:16 (ICB)

In the previous chapter, I listed music experiences as one of several
activities that enhance interest and give opportunities to practice
character virtues and spiritual disciplines. In this chapter, I expand on the importance and the use of this powerful tool.

I would have you know that even though I use music extensively
with children, music is not my strength. I enjoy and appreciate various
forms of music, I am able to play a tape recorder and a CD player, and
I can push the buttons on an autoharp. So I write this chapter in hopes
of encouraging you, no matter your skill or lack of skill, to make music
a large part of your overall character development strategy.

The Power of Music

Music is a universal tool for communicating ideas, emotions, and attitudes. When words are added to music, the intellect is touched as well as the emotions. The combination of rhythm, rhyme (lyrics), and melody forms one of the most powerful teaching tools in existence—a song.

Often a song becomes so indelibly imprinted in the minds and hearts of people (both young and old) that it literally cannot be forgotten. How important it is, then, for parents, teachers, and leaders involved in children's character and spiritual formation to use songs to aid children in their character growth.

The variety of music-oriented experiences you may make available to children is almost endless. Because singing is the most familiar music activity, I want to begin by considering it first.

Selecting Appropriate Songs

The story is told of a family driving home from church whose third grade girl began flapping her arms and making sounds like a machine gun. This behavior seemed rather unusual to her father, who began to listen more closely and then heard his daughter singing, "...fly over the enemy, shoot the artillery...." The father, with curiosity fully aroused, asked a few questions. He learned that his daughter was singing about being "in the Lord's army," a song that had been sung in Sunday school with great enjoyment.

Was this song appropriate for her to be singing? Her father didn't think so.

Because of the impact of music on children, leaders and parents need to ask themselves the following questions about the songs they choose to use with children. The goal is to select songs with words that fortify character virtues and spiritual disciplines.

> The goal is to select songs with words that fortify character virtues and spiritual disciplines.

- Is the meaning of the song clear to children? (concrete and age appropriate)

- Is it easy to sing?
- Are the words scripturally and doctrinally correct?
- Does the song build beliefs that drive virtuous behavior?
- Does the song build positive attitudes?
- Does the song relate to the character virtue(s) being developed?
- Does the song fit the present age and culture?

When I apply these questions to the lyrics of the song the little girl's father overheard her singing, the only question that can be answered with a "yes" is that the song is easy to sing.

Learning a New Song

Even when songs are carefully selected for appropriateness, the task of learning new songs is a very real problem for many teachers and parents. The problem affects those who lack confidence in their own singing voices and those who find it difficult to decipher an unfamiliar melody, especially if they do not read music or are in classroom settings without an accompanist. If any of the above descriptions fit you, keep in mind that musical excellence is not essential in providing good musical experiences for children. In fact, children more readily identify with an ordinary voice than with a highly trained beauty.

To learn a new song, try one or more of these ideas:

- Find a friend who likes to sing who will teach you the song, or ask a friend who plays an instrument to play the melody for you.
- Use a cassette/CD/iPod to record your friend's music, or secure a professional recording of the song. Play it over and over until you can sing the song easily.
- Keep in mind that recorded voices need to be simple, natural, and in the same key children sing. Accompaniment needs to be soft enough to allow the words, melody, and rhythm all to come through clearly.
- Meet with other teachers or parents to practice the song until you can all sing it easily and confidently.

Introducing a New Song

After you have mastered a new song, your task is to present it effectively to your children. Try these ideas for introducing a new song to your children:

- Letter the song's words on a chart or on PowerPoint slides.
- Learn the song well, and then sing the song to the children without accompaniment.
- Introduce the new song simply by giving children the opportunity to listen to it once or twice. Give them something specific to listen for, e.g., "Count the number of ways the song says to show compassion."
- Show pictures or objects to illustrate the song's words.
- Discuss what was heard, and then sing the song together.

Perhaps this song about forgiveness is new to you. Take a moment to think about how you would accomplish some of these ideas using this song.

I-M-U-R-F-O-R-G-I-V-E-N

(I Am, You Are Forgiven)

Lyrics and Music by Douglas C. Eltzroth*

One, two, three, four
I-M-U-R
F-O-R-G-I-V-E-N
I-M-I-M-F-O-R-G-I-V-E-N
I-M-I-M-F-O-R-G-I-V-E-N
I-M-I-M
That is why I sing and shout
That is why I dance about
I-M-I-M-F-O-R-G-I-V-E-N

I agreed with God
That I'd done something wrong
I believed and He forgave
And gave to me this song

F-O-R-G-I-V-E-N
U-R-U-R-F-O-R-G-I-V-E-N
U-R-U-R-F-O-R-G-I-V-E-N
U-R-U-R

Now it's time to sing and shout   F-O-R-G-I-V-E-N
Now it's time to dance about   I-M-I-M-F-O-R-G-I-V-E-N
U-R-U-R-F-O-R-G-I-V-E-N   I-M-I-M-F-O-R-G-I-V-E-N
I confessed to God   I-M-I-M
That I'd done something
wrong
I believed and He forgave
And gave to me this song

* Used by permission. From "It Takes Love" music cassette, available through Character Choice, www.characterchoice.org.

More Music Experience Ideas

Try incorporating some additional music activities that you may not have tried yet. Here are just a few.

Guide children in singing antiphonally by having them repeat the exact phrase after you have sung it. Begin by dividing children into two groups. One group sings a phrase, and then the second group sings a phrase.

Group 1: Come and praise the Lord our King,
Group 2: Hallelujah!
Group 1: Lift your voice and let us sing,
Group 2: Hallelujah!

Another music activity is illustrating the song or making a rebus chart of the words. A rebus chart is a graphic display of the song that replaces some of the words with pictures, which enables beginning readers to learn the song's words quickly.[1]

There are also music listening activities that teach many other skills besides musical ones. As a song is played, ask the children to listen to the music and words. As it is played again, ask them to draw a picture that shows what they see in their minds or what their attitude is as they listen.

Children of all ages enjoy writing words to a melody. Some children enjoy composing their own melody and words. It is easier to begin this type of music experience by writing words to an existing tune. For a variety, select familiar tunes, popular songs, or television commercial tunes. Guide children to create words that reflect character virtue ideas.

Here are a couple of songs written to reflect specific character virtues that have been set to familiar tunes.

COMPASSION SONG (Tune: "Mary Had a Little Lamb")

Have compassion, learn to care,   Have compassion, give your best,
Learn to share, everywhere.   Nothing less, just say, "Yes!"
Have compassion, help someone,   Have compassion, help someone,
God's love and work is done.   Then God's love and work is done.

IT'S BEST TO FORGIVE (Tune: "The Farmer in the Dell")

God forgives us all.   It's best to forgive.
God forgives us all.   It's best to forgive. "I was wrong"
He loves us and we love Him,   Say "I'll forgive" and give a hug.
God forgives us all.   It's best to forgive.

Transition rhymes for young children give the opportunity to exercise large muscles and move from one activity to another. Using guided conversation with transition rhymes creates the added benefit of labeling, practicing, and fortifying a virtue. The "Open, Shut Them" rhyme helps children practice being responsible listeners by giving them concrete, fun ways to focus their hands, minds, and bodies.

Guided conversation using this transition rhyme would sound like this: "Let's prepare our hands, minds, and bodies to be *responsible* listeners by saying the 'Open, Shut Them' rhyme." Hold both hands up, palms out, facing the children, and repeat the rhyme:

Open, shut them, (open and shut your hands as you say these words)
Open, shut them,
Give a little clap. (clap once)
Open, shut them,
Open, shut them,
Lay them in your lap. (clasp your hands together and place them in your lap)

Another transition rhyme to use after children have been sitting and listening is "Wiggle." This rhyme is a familiar one. Make it a character-building and practicing activity using guided conversation like this: "You have been *responsible* to sit and listen and think so well! Now it is time to stand and wiggle and say a rhyme together. I will say it first, and then you repeat it. Then we will say it together." (Repeat as needed to shake out the "wiggles.")

WIGGLE
(wiggle the body parts as they are mentioned)
Wiggle my fingers,
Wiggle my toes,
Wiggle my nose,
Wiggle my shoulders,
Now no more wiggles are left in me,
So I will sit as still and *respectful* as I can be.

Bible verses set to music are long remembered. Rhythm and melody add to the impact of the words and increase children's retention. A favorite of mine is "Be kind and tender hearted, forgiving one another, remembering the way that God has forgiven you."[2]

Instrumental and rhythm experiences also can be incorporated into character-building activities. Some instruments that easily lend themselves for use by children are melody bells, the autoharp, zither, guitar, and rhythm instruments such as music sticks, bells, and castanets. *For use by children* are the key words. Remember, it is the children (not the leaders or parents) whom we want to involve as active participants in using these instruments.

Action songs are important for children because they allow children to move and wiggle. Finger plays are used to allow movement and to access long-term memory. Using rounds and chants, rhythm and movement, and making rhythm instruments create the opportunity to reinforce and internalize character virtues in children.

Music experiences may be used to answer questions and enhance concepts. In Chapter Three, I mentioned using a song to answer questions about the Holy Spirit. Here is that powerful song:

SPIRIT OF GOD
*Lyrics and Music by Douglas C. Eltzroth**
The Spirit of God is my Helper and Guide
Giving me power to do what is right
(Repeat)
Spirit of God - Spirit of God
Spirit of God - Spirit of God
(Repeat)
He gives love - He gives joy
He gives peace - And He gives
Patience to both young and old

Kindness and goodness
And faithfulness, gentleness
He even gives self-control

* Used by permission. From "It Takes Love" music cassette, available through Character Choice, www.characterchoice.org.

Music Listening Experiences

There is great value in having children listen to music as well as involving them in singing or playing music. With all the electronic equipment available these days, listening can be accomplished individually, in a small group, or in a music center.

Have children listen to music to enrich the character virtue upon which you are presently focused. Choose from children's song books, praise choruses, or hymns. For example, the familiar hymn "Trust and Obey" fits the foundation virtues of compassion, respect, and responsibility.

> Have children listen to music to enrich the character virtue upon which you are presently focused.

Help children choose pictures to illustrate the songs. Children may select magazine pictures or create their own. This idea works for any song, but remember to choose songs that relate to the character virtues you are developing.

Finding music that speaks to specific character virtues takes some extra effort. Here are a few sources:

Character Classics, The Legacy Company, 1432 Marsh Lane, 330, Dallas TX 75234

SkyRyder Kids, Tony Salerno, 2648 E. Workman Ave. #305, West Covina, CA 91791

Kathleen Chapman (eleven character virtue songs), www.kathleen-chapman.com

It Takes Love cassette, Character Choice, 1545 Tanaka Dr., Erie, CO 80516

NOTES

[1] Barbara J. Bolton, *How To Do Bible Learning Activities* (Ventura, CA: GL Publications, 1982), 89.

[2] (Ephesians 4:32, song #87, *Sing Praises Music for Children*, Grades 1-6, G/L Publications).

Think on These Things

For the next two days, listen to and list the songs and music you enjoy in your everyday, walk-around "with-God life."

_____

_____

_____

Which of these songs and music selections encourage the growth of positive character in you?

_____

_____

_____

Practice It!

Locate a children's music book. Children's pastors would likely have an early childhood or elementary children's songbook for you to borrow. Review a few of the songs. Or listen to a children's cassette or CD. List the songs that would teach or fortify the positive character virtues you want to develop.

_____

_____

_____

Use the suggestions in this chapter to learn one of these songs and teach it to your children.

CHAPTER ELEVEN

Spiritual Disciplines and Character Formation

*"...to be made new in the attitude of your minds; and to put on the
new self, created to be like God in true righteousness and holiness."*
Ephesians 4:23–24

*"A Spiritual Discipline is an intentionally directed action by which
we do what we can do in order to receive from God the ability (or
power) to do what we cannot do by direct effort."*
The Renovaré Spiritual Formation Bible[1]

Becoming people who reflect God's character requires that we
and the children we serve desire and intentionally discipline
ourselves to the formation of an intimate relationship with God.
The word *discipline* comes directly from the Latin *disciplinia*, meaning
"giving instruction to a disciple."

Introduction to Spiritual Disciplines

In the book *Celebration of Discipline*, Richard Foster identifies twelve
disciplines that, when practiced daily in our ordinary lives, nurture
spiritual maturity and deepen our connection with God. Foster's twelve

spiritual disciplines are: meditation, prayer, fasting, study, simplicity, solitude, submission, service, confession, worship, guidance, and celebration.[2]

The goal of these spiritual disciplines is to put us in a place where the Holy Spirit is able to do God's inner transformation. In this context, discipline requires correction, but it does not involve punishment.

The personal practice of spiritual disciplines invites God to change us, to build His character in us, to make us more like His Son Jesus, and to live a "with-God life." The task for us as children's advocates is to cast the practice of these spiritual disciplines into concrete experiences for our children. We are interpreters of God's book the Bible, His ways, and His character for them. Translating God's ways and character into children's language and experiences that allow their spiritual growth is of primary importance.

While all of these disciplines are essential and not one is more important than the other, the disciplines of meditation, prayer, and simplicity are what we will examine here. I have chosen these three because I believe they are powerful antidotes for the pressure and hectic nature of today's world.

This may be a good place for me to refresh your memory concerning the principles of how children think and learn, covered in Chapter Seven.

Principle One: Children's thinking is limited by their perspective.
Principle Two: Children's thinking depends on the quality and quantity of first hand experiences.
Principle Three: Children's thinking is limited to physical activities.

Keep these principles in mind as you continue on in this chapter.

The Discipline of Meditation

The purpose of meditation is to have a familiar, intimate relationship with God. Richard Foster describes meditation for those who follow

Jesus as "the ability to hear God's voice and obey his word. It is that simple."[3] When I put this idea into children's language, it sounds and looks like the following set of ideas.

Listen to the Words and Ways of God

Listening is a meditation discipline that needs to be practiced. Be creative about times and places to encourage listening. Use teachable moments as well as intentional strategies. Practice listening while riding in the car with the windows open or walking in a park. Encourage children to listen for God's words and ways with questions like, "What need does the rush of traffic sounds and busyness bring

> "Where there is peace and meditation, there is neither anxiety nor doubt."
> –St. Francis of Assisi

to your thoughts?" (A possible answer: the need to ask God for peace in the middle of all the noise and busyness.) Be sure to allow children time to give their thoughts and ideas.

Listening as you walk with children is another way to practice this discipline. As you begin a walk, ask children to close their mouths but open their ears and eyes to look for and listen for creatures God has made. "Look for colors and textures in trees, flowers, insects, animals, sky, and clouds. Think on, or mediate on, what you see and hear. Remember and be ready to talk about what you see and hear when we return."

Listening to music is an easy way to practice meditation. Play music that your children know and enjoy. Instead of singing the music, ask them to stay still, not move or talk, just listen to the words. When finished, ask the children to describe what they were thinking as they listened to the words and music.

Give Children Scripture Truths and Verses to Think On

Children need consistent labeling of their sense of worth, belonging, and competence. Choose Scripture verses that give the truth about their worth. Worth is established by knowing and believing that Jesus willingly gave His life for each and every boy and girl. "Christ died for us" (Romans 5:6a, ICB).

Give children the truth about being a child of God and belonging to Him. "To all who received him [Jesus], who believed in his name, he gave the right to become children of God" (John 1:12). "You are children of God by faith in Christ Jesus" (Galatians 3:26b, ICB).

Give them the truth that competence results from experience and dependence upon the Holy Spirit to teach, help, and guide. "God is working in you, to help you want to do what pleases him. Then he gives you the power to do it" (Philippians 2:13, icb). In teachable moments and in time of choice and conflict, remind children to think (meditate) on these truths.

Give Children Thoughts about Character Virtues

Tell children ways that God shows His character to the world. "God's compassion for the people of the world is so great He sent His Son Jesus to tell them He loves every man, woman, boy, and girl." "God forgives the wrong things people think, say and do." "God always keeps His promises. People who keep promises are people of integrity."

Memorize the Words of God

Make Scripture memorization an intrinsic part of forming the habit of meditation. Select age-appropriate verses, and give children a variety.

Choose verses that give children thoughts of joy and happiness. "God is love" (1 John 4:8). "Praise the lord, for the lord is good" (Psalm 135:3). "God, every morning you hear my voice. Every morning, I tell you what I need. And I wait for your answer" (Psalm 5:3, ICB). "Rejoice in the Lord always. I will say it again: Rejoice!" (Philippians 4:4).

Include verses to counteract peer pressures. "A friend loves at all times" (Proverbs 17:17). "Be kind and loving to each other. Forgive each other just as God forgave you in Christ" (Ephesians 4:32, ICB). "Let's think about each other and help each other to show love and do good deeds" (Hebrews 10:24, ICB).

Today's media and culture are filled with messages of fear and distrust. Choose verses that give children the truth about their security. "I am with you always" (Matthew 28:20). "I will never leave you; I will never forget you" (Hebrews 13:5, icb). "Do not be afraid; do not be discouraged" (Joshua 8:1).

Learn to Read, Use, and Meditate on God's Book the Bible

Help your children become familiar with the Bible. Children are able to learn about the Bible as early as when they are toddlers. Following are two finger plays for toddlers through age three.

The Bible is God's special book (hold Bible)

His Words are written there (open Bible and point to words)

And when I turn each page to look (turn pages)

I handle it with care (hold open in hand)

The Holy Bible is God's book (form book with hands)

Let's open it and see

Where He tells us of His love

He loves you, He loves me (point to others, point to self)

> "I have so much to do today; I need to meditate twice as long."
>
> *–Gandhi*

With four- and five-year-olds, hold a Bible in your hands and ask children to hold out their hands, palms up, and together say: "This is God's book the Bible. The Bible is divided into two parts. The Old Testament (touch the Old Testament side and allow children to repeat 'Old Testament') and the New Testament (touch the New Testament side and allow children to repeat 'New Testament')."

Then say: "The names of the first five books of the Old Testament (start with lifting your thumb, and move to forefinger and on through your little finger as you speak) are Genesis, Exodus, Leviticus, Numbers, Deuteronomy. The names of the first five books of the New Testament (on your other hand, begin with your thumb, and move to forefinger through your little finger as you speak) are Matthew, Mark, Luke, John, Acts." After you say each book's name, allow time for children to repeat the name.

For early elementary age children, add the information that the Bible contains sixty-six books, thirty-nine books in the Old Testament and twenty-seven books in the New Testament.

For older children, make this strategy a fun drill using both the Old Testament and New Testament as described above. Then to the Old Testament, add the books of history, psalms, proverbs, and the prophets. Add to the New Testament the rest of the books (as it is age-level appropriate).

Help elementary age children identify that each book in the Bible has chapters and each chapter has verses. The chapters have the big numbers and the verses have the small numbers.

Create a time when you read aloud a meaningful, age-level appropriate portion of God's book the Bible. Read with thought to your tone of voice and inflection and interest. Psalms and the Gospels are a good place to start. Read out of a children's version. Ask the children to listen as you read and be ready to share their thoughts when you finish.

Train children to use their imagination while listening to a passage of Scripture. Think of helping them learn the ancient tradition called *lectio divina*. Marti Watson describes the use of *lectio divina* with children:

> Because *lectio divina* is a slow and measured reading, choose an active story from the Bible, such as Daniel and the lion's den. Read the story aloud in a hushed and reverential way. Ask your children what stands out, providing adequate think-time. Children must be helped to approach the Bible this way; it doesn't come naturally to any of us. And remember, there are no right or wrong answers.
>
> After all have had a chance to respond, read the story aloud again. This time ask what the setting looked like, what the lions sounded like, what the expressions on Daniel's face was when he was thrown in the den, what the king and his court looked liked, and so on. Finally, read the story aloud one additional time, and then give everyone a chance to share what he or she heard as a personal message from the story. One person may hear the need for courage, while another may hear the need to trust God in the face of death.[3]

As always, modeling is one of the most effective methods of training and practice. So begin by becoming comfortable with your own meditative ability. Inevitability your comfortableness will grow as you prepare and practice with children.

The Discipline of Prayer

Prayer may be a new experience for you as well as for the children you are teaching. Teacher and parent examples are more powerful in teaching prayer than anything said about prayer.

Become a model of prayer as a natural part of life. Jesus modeled prayer as an integral part of His everyday experiences. Sometimes Jesus' prayers were formal, head bowed, eyes closed. Sometimes He prayed as He walked and talked with the people and His disciples. Many times He prayed with individuals, sometimes with small groups, and sometimes with very large groups of people. Often He prayed alone.

Be spontaneous with your prayers, and pray about everything. Pets and parking places are concrete, everyday stuff. When I broke my left arm, six months later had rotator surgery on the right arm, and a year later broke my left leg, my grandchildren heard me ask God for close parking places due to the injuries. Now that I am recovered, my prayer for parking places has changed to, "Please help us find a parking place that is best for our health and gives those who aren't so healthy the close places."

At the sound of sirens, pray for the drivers of the vehicles, those who may be injured, paramedics, and doctors. In doing so, you allow children to observe that prayer is something you value and like to do. These types of prayers influence children's attitudes about prayer.

Develop a Pattern of Prayer That Is Age Appropriate

In your home in the mornings, make it possible for your children to hear and see you pray. Pray at mealtimes using different prayers and prayer songs. Pray with your children at bedtime.

In the classroom, consider beginning your class time with prayer. If you are teaching in public school, it may not be a choice to do so out loud, but you may invite the children to a moment of silence as you pray silently for the needs in your classroom.

Pray with children before their sporting or club events. Pray for coaches, referees, judges, and children to be honest and attitudes to be respectful and responsible.

In preschool, pray at snack time. Encourage children to teach each other the prayers they pray in their home. Ending time is often a time to model prayers of thanksgiving and compassion for needs that have surfaced during class.

Make Prayer Simple and Short

Many adult prayers convince children that prayer is difficult and boring. Make yours simple. At meals and snack time: "For health and strength and daily food we praise Your name, Lord." For bedtime/ending times: "Thank You for Your loving care round about us everywhere." Then you and your children may each pray spontaneous thank-you or blessings prayers.

Here are a couple of songs that help teach and model prayer to children.

I ASKED GOD

Lyrics and Music by Douglas C. Eltzroth*

I asked God for something special
And He said "Yes, that's a green
light. Go!"
I asked God for something special.
He said "Yes" not no.

(CHORUS)

Because He loves me and knows
what
is very best for me. (Repeat)

I asked God for something special.
And He said "No, that's a red light.
Stop."
I asked God for something special
He said "Absolutely not!"

(CHORUS)

I asked God for something special.
And He said
"Wait, that's a yellow light. Slow."
I asked God for something special.
And He will let me know.

(CHORUS)

Sometimes He gives answers,
Not red or yellow or green.
Much better than I asked for,
Much better than my dreams.
It was not on my prayer list.
He thought it up for me.
Much better than I hoped for.
Exactly what I need!!

*Used by permission.

I CAN TALK TO GOD

Lyrics and Music by Douglas C. Eltzroth*

I can talk to God anytime,
I can talk to God anywhere
We can talk about anything,
And He hears my prayer
He's always there,
Anytime, I can talk to God
anywhere,
We can talk about anything
And He hears my prayer, He's always there.
He always hears my prayer
I can talk to God with my seatbelt on
I can talk to God when my Mom is gone
I can talk to God when my friend
can't play
It doesn't matter what time of day
I can talk to God if I'm bowing my head
I can talk to God if I'm laying in bed
I can talk to God just running around
It doesn't matter if I'm up or down
And the list goes on and on and on
and on and on

(Refrain)
I can talk to God when I'm climbing
a tree
I can talk to God down on my knees
I can talk to God right before a meal
It doesn't matter about the way I feel
I can talk to God if I'm feeling sad
I can talk to God when I'm really mad
I can talk to God when I'm afraid of the
night
It doesn't matter if it's dark or light
And the list goes on and on and on
and on and on

(Refrain)
I can talk to God when I'm
singing a song
I can talk to God just walking along
I can talk to God about the
problems I've had
It doesn't matter if it's good or bad
I can talk to God about surprise things
I can talk to God about everything
I can talk to God, Oh yes I can and
It doesn't matter if its' anyplace, anybody,
Anyhow, anymore, anyone,
anything
Anyway, anytime, any old "any." at all
(Refrain)

*Used by permission.

When you are praying aloud with children, focus your prayer on the virtue(s) you are developing. "Dear forgiving God, thank You for talking to us. Thank You for being compassionate with us. Thank You for forgiving us when we tell You we have thought, said, or done wrong things. Help us to choose to forgive ourselves and others. Thank You for always loving and forgiving us. In Jesus' name we pray, amen."

An important part of prayer is listening to God. Following is an interaction I use for guiding children to listen to God. It incorporates the principle on how children think and learn related to physical experiences. I have used it with children as young as four and as old as ten.

Prayer is talking to God. But sometimes it is right and good to listen quietly to God. Prayer is also listening to God. Here is a fun way to prepare to listen.

First, we will make noise and then make quiet so we are ready to hear what God has to say to us. Please stand and make noise by clapping your hands as loud as you can and stomping your feet until I say stop. Ready? Go! Make noise. (Allow children to make noise for 30 to 45 seconds.)

Stop. Now make quiet. Begin by sitting down. No sounds at all until I say stop. Ready? Go! Make quiet. (Allow children to make quiet for 30 to 45 seconds. Repeat this pattern again, increasing the times to 60 to 75 seconds.)

As we continue to make quiet, listen for what God is saying to you. (Pause and allow time for listening.) If you would like to share with all of us what God is saying to you, please do so now. (Pause and allow responses from children. Do not force any reply. Trust the Holy Spirit to speak to and through the children.)

A prayer chart is another way to help the experience of prayer become concrete. The chart needs to be simple and easy for children to use.

My Prayer List

"Do not be anxious about anything, but in everything by prayer and petition, with thanksgiving, present your request to God."
Philippians 4:6

What I Am Praying About	Date I Began to Pray	On This Date God Said...
_____	_____	_____
_____	_____	_____
_____	_____	_____
_____	_____	_____

The Discipline of Simplicity

Of great concern to me as a children's advocate is our culture's demand that we have more and more. We can never seem to have enough. David Elkind wrote in his 2001 edition of *The Hurried Child,* "Parents are under more pressure than ever to overschedule their children and have them engage in organized sports and other activities that may be age-inappropriate. Unhappily, the overtesting of children in public schools has become more extensive than it was even a decade ago. In some communities even kindergarteners are given standardized tests. Media pressures to turn children into consumers have also grown exponentially."[4]

Children's celebrations are an example. They are driven by the biggest, the best, and outdoing the last celebration. Birthday parties that once consisted of inviting friends for ice cream, cake, and simple presents are now celebrated with clowns, tents, deejays, and extravagant gifts. Graduations, which were once the privilege of those completing high school or college, now begin in kindergarten.

In the mid 1990s, I re-entered the U.S. culture after serving as a teacher and trainer for five years in the former Soviet Union. My culture shock took many forms, but the part that grieved me the most was to see the marketing that was being done to children. Here are just a few examples that startled me: the obsession with owning the latest Beanie Baby; the race to McDonald's for the latest Happy Meal toy; the designer fashions for children; and children's status being measured by the school attended, the sports they were doing, and their labeled clothing. Something that was amazing to me for all ages was the rise of the "collectables" market. Children's shelves and closets were filled with stuff!

We all have stuff! Many of us hang onto things that need to go: clothes we haven't worn in years, magazines that someone has convinced us need to be saved forever, and books that will never be read. Instead of following the way of the culture, choose to model the habit of giving away clothing that is no longer worn and borrowing books and magazines from a library instead of purchasing them.

Recently I was told of a conversation between a twenty-something girl and a forty-something woman concerning the purchasing of clothes. The younger lady was excitedly showing her friend her new clothes. The older woman asked, "Which of your present clothing items are you going to give away as a result of these purchases?"

The younger woman replied, "What do you mean?"

"I make it a rule," replied the older but wiser woman, "to give away an article of clothing for each new one I purchase. It helps me be conscious of the need of keeping some degree of simplicity in my life."

The puzzled reply was, "I have never been taught or encouraged to simplify anything. Why is simplicity something you desire?"

Richard Foster states the reason for simplicity the best. "Simplicity is freedom. The discipline of simplicity is an inward reality that results in an outward life-style."[5]

Practicing a simpler lifestyle is a difficult task in our culture. Somehow it is wrong to wear clothes or drive cars until they are worn out. But it is possible to reorient our lives through simplicity so that possessions can be genuinely enjoyed without destroying us. It takes purposeful strategies and practice to keep our focus on choosing the simple life. Children best learn this discipline from what is demonstrated.

Practicing the discipline of simplicity creates the opportunity to practice compassion, responsibility, integrity, and perseverance. Here are some ideas to jump-start your thinking:

- Evaluate the ways you are spending time to see if you are doing so responsibly. Time is such a gift. Are you and your children slaves to the clock? How often do your children hear the words "we don't have time to..." or "I'm so busy" or "I do not have time to sit and talk with my family"?

- No is okay! You do not have to explain or have an excuse for why you are saying no. It is not only acceptable to say, "No, this is not the right time," but it is a matter of being a person of integrity.

- Simplify possessions. Each time you purchase a new piece of clothing for your children, help them give one piece of clothing they have not worn for the past year to a family or charity in need. Label this giving as an act of compassion. Find activities that they can participate in without needing specialized equipment, clothing, or fees.

- Create a field trip to the city dump or recycling center to learn how to conserve the world's resources. Make recycling of cans, newspapers, and other items that can be used again by others a family or school project. This idea becomes a way to practice the virtues of compassion and responsibility.

- Spend time helping children eliminate clutter. Apply this idea to children's personal spaces in classrooms and at home. Help them identify how having too many possessions makes life burdensome. When drawers, cubbies, lockers, and closets are cleaned out, it is easier to find items. When things are organized, time and effort is saved in locating what is wanted. Make the cleanout process a low-key, scheduled event. In a school environment, it might happen at the beginning, middle, and ending of a school day or before holidays or school breaks. At home, the removal of clutter event might take place on birthdays or before or after family visits. Label these tasks as opportunities to practice perseverance.

- Have a discussion with children about the activities they are or want to be involved in. Is an activity something they are doing to please a parent, teacher, or coach rather than what is truly what they want to experience? At the first opportunity,

guide children to eliminate any activities they are not passionate about. Be sure to give them encouragement for becoming a
responsible person.

- Is your community one where each birthday party has to be
  larger and splashier than the previous one? Then make a difference by returning to a simpler event. Most likely it will take
  some perseverance to do so. Help children think of simpler
  ways. Perhaps the guests may make their own ice cream sun-
  daes. If it is summer and hot, fill balloons with water for a
  gentle, benevolent, fun water fight.

Through the practice of the discipline of simplicity, there is hope
for people to rediscover meaningful relationships with others, a life less
cluttered, the living out of simple virtues, and release from the tyranny
of "muchness and manyness."

NOTES

[1] Richard Foster et al. *The Renovaré Spiritual Formation Bible* (San Francisco: Harper-
Collins, 2005), *xxxiv.*

[2] Richard Foster, *Celebration of Discipline* (San Francisco: HarperCollins, 1998), 17.
Ibid.

[3] Marti Watson and Valerie Hess, *Habits of a Child's Heart* (Colorado Springs, CO:
NavPress, 2004), 29.

[4] David Elkind, *The Hurried Child*, 3d ed. (Cambridge, Mass: Perseus Publishing,
2001), *xv.*

[5] Richard Foster, *Celebration of Discipline,* 3d ed. (San Francisco: HarperCollins, 1998),
79.

Think on These Things

Chose one of the three spiritual disciplines presented in this chapter to practice for the next week. Write your choice here: _____

_____

What is your motive for further exploring this discipline?

_____

_____

Where in your everyday, walk-around life are you practicing (or not) this discipline?

_____

_____

_____

What character virtue(s) will help you accomplish the practice of this discipline? Circle one or more: compassion, forgiveness, integrity, respect, responsibility, initiative, cooperation, perseverance.

Practice It!

Create an intentional strategy for your children to introduce and practice the spiritual discipline you have chosen to practice.

_____

_____

_____

_____

Pray continually for God's character to drive your inner discipline and spiritual strength to meet each challenge or difficulty that keeps you from entering into the habits of the spiritual disciplines.

CHAPTER TWELVE

Guiding Children to an Intimate, Personal Life with God

"I loved you as the Father loved me. Now remain in my love."
(John 15:9, ICB)

The following appeared in an article on *Monday, July 16, 2007,* in Today's Children's Ministry Newsletter-HTML. It begins with a question from someone using a secular character education curriculum.

"Our program and your children's ministry are really trying to do the same thing, right?"

An interesting question, for sure. And a wrong one.

It came from someone who organizes programs for kids to help them develop positive character traits. I'm [*sic*] definitely all in favor of guiding children in character and morality growth—I'm a parent, after all. But I had to disagree with this person. The words of C.S. Lewis in *Mere Christianity* explain why:

"We must not suppose that even if we succeeded in making everyone nice we should have saved their souls. A world of nice people, content in their own niceness, looking no further, turned away from God, would be just as desperately in need of salvation as a miserable world—and might even be more difficult to save."

The writer of this article is pointing out a serious flaw in some character development efforts, which is the idea that children's character can be formed and transformed in the image of God apart from the work of the Holy Spirit in their lives. Character formation and transformation require an inward working of God's spirit upon a person's spirit. As we guide the formation of God's character in children, we also are guiding the formation of their spiritual lives. This privilege includes introducing them to the person of God, life with God, and an intimate relationship with God through His Son Jesus, with the help and power of the Holy Spirit.

Developing positive character virtues apart from a personal relationship with God is arguably possible to some degree, but living out God's character in relationships, communities, and societies requires the inner presence and power of God's spirit.

The Role of Community in a Child's Personal Life with God

A child's personal life with God and His Son Jesus is a sensitive area in the thinking of those concerned with children's spiritual development. How early in life is it possible for children to be aware of life with God? To talk to and hear God's voice? To respond to the Holy Spirit's prompting to invite Jesus into their lives?

Much of the disagreement on this question seems to be focused on the age or stage of development at which children are considered to be accountable for their decisions and actions. Perhaps it is the mental and emotional age of a child and the way in which that child's spiritual life is being developed rather than the chronological age of the child that is a determining factor. A larger factor, however, is the nature of the child's community, which is determined by the character and spiritual life of the key influencers in the child's life.

Community creates the possibility of an atmosphere and environment where children touch, taste, smell, see, and hear the "with-God life." It may become the place where children grow in their understanding of a relationship with Jesus, His Father God, and the Holy Spirit as their helper and guide. A "with-God life" community is a place where children may see and hear their parents, relatives, teachers, coaches, and others reading God's book the Bible and talking with God. Children may take part in asking and answering questions about how God comes to us. They may be involved in identifying the beauty and intelligence of His creation. And children may learn by example and guidance to trust and obey and be people of compassion, forgiveness, and integrity.

The family is the child's primary community. Family community is where parents live out the covenant relationship they are instructed by God to keep with their children: "Love GOD, your God, with your whole heart: love him with all that's in you, love him with all you've got! Write these commandments that I've given you today on your hearts. Get them inside of you and then get them inside your children. Talk about them wherever you are, sitting at home or walking in the street; talk about them from the time you get up in the morning to when you fall into bed at night. Tie them on your hands and foreheads as a reminder; inscribe them on the doorposts of your homes and on your city gates" (Deuteronomy 6:5–9, MSG).

Sadly, many families have not been privileged to be instructed or to learn to live the "with-God life." Other communities that may contribute to guiding the formation of a child's character and spiritual life include community resource centers, schools, churches, synagogues, Sunday school programs, confirmand classes, communicant classes, catechism classes, and synagogue classes.

The role of these communities is crucial in providing instruction, training, practice, and modeling. In a multicultural society such as ours where family structures vary widely, the task is huge. The structure of families may very, but the possibility of living and modeling life with God is a reality for all families. The goal for those who lead children and families in these communities is character and spiritual formation into the likeness of Christ. Then the leaders disciple those they serve in character and spiritual formation.

George Gallup has said, "I think people want to grow in their experience of community and grow in their faith, but often they don't know how. They don't know the practical steps or how to live out these religious ["with-God life"] experiences in their lives."[1]

The purpose of all with-God communities is to have children understand that God is with them and He always desires to love and care for them and in return for them to love Him. The communities are to tell the true story of God sending His Son Jesus to make it possible for people, men and women and boys and girls, to live with God now and forever. The communities are also responsible to guide children to a time when they make a personal choice to invite God to not only be with them but to live in them.

Building Children's Attitudes and Understanding about a Personal Life with God

In his book *Teaching Your Child About God, You Can't Begin Too Soon*,[2] Wes Haystead challenges parents and teachers who are followers of Jesus to make "a careful analysis of what children actually do think about God, how they develop their concepts, and ways of helping to prepare them for more mature understanding." In other words, the concerns of us who serve children in their character and spiritual formation are to be focused on listening to what children are thinking about God and guiding and shaping their attitudes and understanding as they grapple with abstract concepts about God, Jesus, and the Holy Spirit.

My years of experience with children of all ages tell me that we can't begin too soon to build a child's attitudes and understanding about an everyday, walk-around life with God. Our first task is to guide them into the awareness of a world filled with God and the promise of a personal relationship with God through His Son Jesus.

My concern is that those of us who are committed to developing the spiritual life of children and their character and conscience toward God have this all-important understanding: guiding children to an intimate, personal "with-God life" is much more than helping children pray a prayer to invite Jesus into their life.

A child's personal relationship with God begins with building positive attitudes and understanding about a compassionate friendship with God based on His love, His desire to live with His created people, and His forgiveness. Then, when the Holy Spirit impresses a child to make a personal decision to invite Jesus into his or her life, it is done so without

> Guiding children to an intimate, personal, "with-God life" is much more than helping children pray a prayer to invite Jesus into their life.

pressure from others. Following a child's decision, intentional guidance and encouragement for the child is needed as the child's "with-God life" continues.

The simple word for salvation in the New Testament is *life*. "I have come that they may have life, and have it to the full," says John 10:10. "He who has the Son has life" (1 John 5:12). Our task as children's advocates, therefore, is to view the development of a child's spiritual "life" as a continuing, ongoing, growing, interactive relationship with Him. This relationship begins *before* children invite Jesus into their life and continues *after* the point of decision.

Parents, teachers, and leaders who want to guide their children into a relationship with God have the responsibility to ask questions, on an ongoing basis, that allow children to describe their understanding, attitudes, and questions about God. In doing so, they must be careful not to ask yes or no questions and questions that put words in a child's mouth. Listen to the interaction between a wise father and his son that follows. Ask yourself how you would have responded if you were the parent.

Five-year-old Simon's father was pleased but surprised when his son announced, "Dad, I want to ask Jesus to come into my life." Simon's dad responded, "I am glad that you are thinking about this, Simon, because it is the most important decision you will make in your life. What do you like most about Jesus?"

Wisely, Simon's father asked this less threatening question rather than asking, "Why do you want Jesus to come into your life?" so it was easier for Simon to answer. And, his father hoped the question would reveal some of Simon's thoughts, attitudes, emotions, and understanding about Jesus.

"I like how He let a boy and his lunch help Him feed all those people," replied Simon.

"That is one way Jesus showed people that He cares and loves them," said Simon's father. "What are some other things you like about Him?"

Simon mentioned how Jesus woke up the little girl and how He had talked to the children even when His helpers tried to stop the children from seeing Him. Finally Simon mentioned that he liked Jesus because Jesus loved everybody. "That is good thinking, Simon," his father said. "I like our life with Jesus. I love Jesus because I know He loves me."

"I love Jesus too," said Simon.

"Let's tell Jesus that we love Him," said Simon's father. After a very simple prayer by father and son, Simon's dad asked, "Simon, would you like to talk more about this now, or would you like to talk about it tonight at bedtime?"

"Later, Dad!" Simon replied and ran outside.

As he thought about his conversation with his son, Simon's father recognized that Simon had not told him anything about personally relating to Jesus or Jesus personally relating to him other than the simple statement that Simon loved Jesus.

When preparing Simon for bed, his father asked him, "Do you remember our conversation this afternoon about you and Jesus? Would you like to talk about Him some more before bedtime?" Simon said that he did, so his father continued. "Today we talked about loving Jesus. What do people do when they love another person very much?"

Simon was quiet for a moment and then said, "They talk and play with each other. They are kind and they say and do things that make them happy."

"Right," his dad said. "Now what happens when people say or do something to a person they love that hurts them or causes them to be unhappy?"

"Well, I guess they need to apologize and tell them you were wrong."

His dad looked straight into Simon's eyes and said, "I am going to ask you a hard question. Have you ever said or done anything that hurt or caused Jesus to be unhappy?"

This question allowed Simon to tell the truth about several acts that he felt were wrong. It was then easy for his dad to lead Simon to pray a prayer in which Simon apologized to Jesus and agreed with Him that what he had thought, said, and done was wrong. The conversation ended by the father saying, "Simon, Jesus loves you so very much. He loves you when you think and say and do right, and He loves you when you think and say and do wrong. I am sure He really likes it when you apologize and ask Him to forgive you. Jesus wants to have a friendship and life with you. He likes to talk with you and play with you. He always loves you and always forgives you. Let's talk about this again in a few days."

This conversation had indicated to his father that Simon knew the difference between right and wrong, and that he had an awareness of how his actions affected others. Most important, Simon had indicated that he wanted to choose the right thing instead of the wrong.

In the next conversation on the subject of Simon's personal relationship with Jesus, his father asked him, "Why do people need to invite Jesus into their lives?" Simon shrugged his shoulders and said he was not sure. Simon's dad explained to him how Jesus wants to love and help people to choose to be and do right things instead of being and doing wrong.

Simon's father brought up the question again several days later. In this interaction, Simon explained in his five-year-old language his need to be forgiven. To be sure that Simon was not just repeating words he had heard, his dad rephrased the question. "What happens when someone invites Jesus into his life?" This question required some help from his dad in stating the answer, and again the subject was held over for another day.

Each time the two discussed Simon inviting Jesus into his life, Simon's father was careful to ask Simon if he wanted to talk about it. If not, he assured Simon that anytime he did want to talk, he would be willing. Whenever Simon would use "Christian language" such as "into my heart," "saved," and "born again," his father would ask Simon to explain what those words meant. He continued to guide Simon's awareness and understanding of everyday, walk-around life with Jesus. Whenever his dad discerned the need to clarify an idea for Simon, he would bring up that idea in the next conversation to check Simon's understanding of the idea or word.

When Simon and his father eventually knelt down and Simon specifically asked Jesus to forgive him for the wrong things he had thought, said, and done and invited Jesus to come into his life, the moment was memorable. But it was not the first time they had prayed to Jesus about a relationship and life with Him. And it wasn't the last. Simon's father continued to talk with his son about life with God through His Son Jesus. This wise father was equally as concerned with Simon's character and conscience formation, his spiritual life, and his growing friendship with Jesus as he had been in helping Simon make his own, clearly understood invitation and commitment to a "with-God life."

What impressed you most about the words Simon's father used when talking with Simon? What jumped out at you about the father's actions and behavior toward his son during their discussions?

The Big Picture—Laying a Solid Foundation

The story of five-year-old Simon and his father illustrates the need to view the formation of a child's character, conscience, and spiritual life as a lifelong opportunity. At the same time, it is good to keep in mind that as a teacher, neighbor, leader, or friend, you may be the only person in a child's life who tells the child the true story of Jesus. My own life story is a testimony to this fact.

I grew up in a home where the only formation toward God as a young child came because I was occasionally sent to Sunday school. Later, when I was in elementary school, my brother took my sister and me to Sunday school, mostly to escape for a few hours the debauchery at our home.

At the age of twelve, I still was escaping the environment of my home by attending a Sunday school that met in a Quonset hut on an Air Force base in northern California. My teacher's name was

Mrs. Allen. I don't remember a lot about the lessons she taught us, but I do remember that I knew she loved me. And she knew how to help me understand God's love for me and guide me to choose to invite Jesus into my life.

Mrs. Allen knew that I would be gone from her influence within six months after my decision because of the nature of Air Force life. In those six short months, she taught me three disciplines that carried me through my teen years. One was to talk to God every day, any time, anywhere. Two was to read and memorize the Bible. And three was to be in community with people who were followers of Jesus.

How about you? Did you invite Jesus into your life as a child or young person? Who helped lay the foundation, and who provided ongoing help and community in your character and spiritual formation?

It is imperative for those of us who are privileged to guide the formation of character and conscience and the spiritual life of children to understand the whole picture—preparation of children to make a decision for Christ, guiding them without pressure to invite Jesus into their life and continued guidance in a "with-God life" that brings spiritual formation—rather than just viewing a "salvation moment" as the first and foremost experience. At the same time, it behooves us to equip ourselves to be able to explain abstract spiritual concepts and give careful attention to language that lays the foundation to help children make a personal decision to invite Jesus into their life.

The consequences of children not having a solid foundation and the whole picture of what it means to have a relationship with Jesus are tragic. "I've been saved seven times." "I got saved at camp this year. Every year at camp I get saved." "I accepted Jesus yesterday, but I want to do it again today." These are testimonies of children who have been in Sunday school, backyard Bible clubs, children's Bible story hours, and other meetings for children. They demonstrate lack of understanding, lack of a solid foundation, and lack of careful use of language by those in a position to help children in the development of

> The consequences of children not having a solid foundation and the whole picture of what it means to have a relationship with Jesus are tragic.

their spiritual life. They also show how children become confused by well-intentioned efforts.

Here are some general ideas and guidelines to use with children in building their understanding of a life with God, the choice to invite Jesus to live in them, and the ongoing, lifelong process of forming their character and spiritual life:

- Avoid abstract terminology. Christians tend to speak another language when they talk about God. Some people call it "Christianese." Think with me about some words and phrases that are commonly used to describe life with God, Jesus, or the experience of salvation. Here is a short list.

Jesus is Lord	Coming into God's family
Father God	Take Jesus into my heart
Salvation	Saved
born again	Accept Jesus as Savior
believe	Receive Christ

  Can you begin to see how confusing these abstract words and phrases are for children?

- Avoid the use of symbols. Use words that mean what they say. Be careful that the real message of God is not hidden in symbolic ideas. Sin is not a black thread or black heart. Sin is lying, stealing, cheating, and so on. Jesus does not come into our hearts, livers, or through doors. Jesus comes into our life. His spirit joins with our spirit (see John 14:17).

- Explain meanings of words. Ask questions to find out the level of children's understanding of words, and then give them age-appropriate explanations that guide them to awareness of Jesus telling us that God loves us and is with us now. When children begin to understand key words such as *believe, sin, salvation, forgiveness,* and *everlasting life,* the foundation is laid for the decision to ask Jesus to live with them and in them.

Please remember that children often imitate or repeat words used by adults to gain acceptance, but their real understanding is based on continual and consistent explanation. The story of Carlos is just one example.

"I want to ask Jesus to live in me again," nine-year-old Carlos said to his teacher one day. "What do you mean ask Jesus to live with you again?" Mr. Hansen replied. "When did you pray and invite Jesus into your life before now?" "When I was at Vacation Bible School this summer," replied Carlos. "Well, Carlos, did you mean it when you asked God to forgive you for the wrong things you think, say, and do? And do you believe that Jesus is God's Son?" said Mr. Hansen. "Yes," replied Carlos, "I believe Jesus is God's Son, and I asked Him to come live in me, but I have thought and said and done some wrong things since then. So, I think I need to ask Jesus to live in me again."

Mr. Hansen realized that Carlos did not understand what asking Jesus to live with him and in him meant. He took time to tell Carlos how to talk to God and to agree with God that what he thought or said or did was wrong and then ask God to forgive him. He helped Carlos read 1 John 1:9 (icb), "But if we confess our sins, he will forgive our sins. We can trust God. He does what is right. He will make us clean from all the wrongs we have done."

- Explain abstract concepts. Since many concepts relating to the Christian faith are very abstract, we can help children visualize these concepts by using physical and concrete terms in our explanations. To help us begin to think about ways to talk us-

What does it mean?
Sin
Savior
Forgive
Trust
Prayer
Faith
Confess
With-God life

ing the language of children, look first at this list of concept words that are often used and heard by children.

Sin	Trust	Confess
Savior	Prayer	Spirit
Forgive	Faith	With-God life

Our task is to find concrete words and ways to illustrate with firsthand experiences or physical activities the meanings of these abstract concepts to children. To do so, we must evaluate our ideas with the three principles discussed in Chapter Seven for understanding how children think and learn.

Principle One: Children's thinking is limited by their perspective.

Principle Two: Children's thinking depends on the quality and quantity of firsthand experiences.

Principle Three: Children's thinking is limited to physical activities.

Following are possible definitions and explanations for the words in the above list:

Sin—"Sin involves thinking, saying, and doing things that God tells us in His book the Bible not to think, say, or do such as lying, stealing, and cheating." (These examples demonstrate Principle Two by using firsthand experiences in the explanation.)

Savior—Children may hear this word but think of the word *saver.* Jesus is a "saver." He puts His money in His piggy bank. To counter this possible misunderstanding, begin your explanation with a firsthand experience of a person such as a lifeguard or fireman. You might say: "Lifeguards and firemen sometimes keep people from dying. Jesus is the Savior. He makes it possible for people to live forever." Remember that children may have experienced someone's death, and you need to clarify that people's bodies die but their spirits can live with Jesus forever.

Forgive—"Forgiving is making a choice to excuse or put away pain or punishment for wrong thoughts, words, or actions." An activity (using Principal One) would be to tell or read a story with an example of someone who made a wrong choice and then was offered forgiveness. Help the children draw or act out the example. Discuss what happened in the story, how the characters might have felt, and the consequences of the actions. Ask the children to share a similar personal experience.

Trust—"To trust means to depend on or to be certain of something or someone." Sitting in a chair is a good firsthand and physical experience for children. All children have the firsthand experience of sitting on a chair that holds them. Trust is built on firsthand experiences that prove true time after time.

Prayer—"Prayer is talking to God, like talking to Mom, Dad, or your friend." A physical/firsthand/visual activity would be a prayer list. Keep the list simple. Use a piece of notebook paper with the heading "I can pray for these people every day." For younger children, gather pictures of people to pray for and glue them on construction paper. Make columns next to the pictures, and have children paste stars or heart stickers next to the person's picture each time they pray.

Faith—Hebrews 11:1 (icb) says, "Faith means being sure of the things we hope for. And faith means knowing that something is real even if we do not see it." We can see that faith is something very difficult to explain to children. One way to explain faith is by asking the question, "Can you think of something that we cannot see but we know is there?" Allow children time to answer. If you need to, ask, "What about the wind?" Allow children time to answer. "We can see the evidence of the wind even though we cannot see it. Faith is the same way. It is a step beyond trust because it involves believing what we cannot understand."

Confess—"To confess means to tell the truth about who God is. To confess also is to agree with God that what I said, thought, or did was not what He wanted." Use the word *confess* as a positive way of saying what is true. "I confess that Jesus is God's Son." This use enables children to develop positive attitudes about talking to God concerning the wrong things that they think, say, or do.

Spirit—that part of you that never dies.

"With-God Life"—"Life with Jesus and God is now and forever. Jesus and God are with you in everything you think and say and do at school, at home, and at a friend's house. Jesus and God are with you in happy and sad times."

- <u>Tell children the source of spiritual concepts.</u> Make sure children are aware that the source of these spiritual words and ideas is the Bible. The Bible is a book written for adults by adults. Adults need to be interpreters of the Bible for children. Be intentional about language and aware of firsthand experiences to relate Bible truths. Whenever possible, open a Bible and point out the verses or words you are reading. Even when a child cannot read, the knowledge and understanding that the words and ideas are from the Bible is important.

- <u>Weave telling children about inviting Jesus to live with them and in them into true stories or in context of Bible stories or Scripture memorization.</u> There are many so-called salvation presentations that may cause children to respond, but these presentations may also just frighten or manipulate them. Here is one of the many stories I have heard concerning what children mistakenly think after hearing an abstract salvation presentation.

A parent phoned me one day and asked if I would be able to meet and talk with her daughter. She said that her child had been crying off and on all night. When asked what was wrong, the daughter said, "I can only tell Ms. Vernie." In conversation with the daughter, she revealed that she had been at a backyard party where a scary clown had said she had to "give her heart to Jesus." "Ms. Vernie, I love Jesus, but if I take a knife and cut out my heart to give to Jesus, I will die."

Before you use a story, ask yourself these questions: Do the words in the story mean what they say? Is the story free from fanciful ideas? How much of the story is actually from the Bible?

An example of a helpful booklet for children is *The Greatest Promise* booklet (see the Appendix).[3] This small booklet is designed to tell the story of Jesus for non-readers through pictures and for beginning readers through reading the text in red. For all others, both the pictures and text give the opportunity to learn about Jesus in children's age-appropriate language and to make the choice to invite Jesus into their life.

When Children Begin to Think and Talk about Inviting Jesus into Their Life

It appears that some children are ready to receive Jesus at a very young age compared with others. Also, parents often discern that one child is more spiritually sensitive than another. We dare not state an age level for any child to receive the Lord Jesus. Nor can we decide to lead "all our class" to decisions. We must keep aware of the fact that it is the Holy Spirit who speaks and draws people to Himself.

The case for children receiving Christ as soon as possible is, however, a strong one. Children are no longer young innocents. They are sophisticated far beyond previous generations. Television, travel, earlier schooling, wider experiences, media, Internet, cell phones, and ipods are stretching their minds, attitudes, and actions. As a result, we can expect children to know the reality of good and evil and to be aware of the pull of sin in their life at a much earlier age.

A young child's decision may be wholehearted and sincere at the moment of the decision. But children are not static beings. They are growing, changing, learning, and thinking. Guiding and helping children explore and discover their own intimate, personal relationship with God after their decision is enhanced when we thoughtfully and carefully answer their questions and create a safe environment where they experience trust and belonging.

Following are precautions to consider when you are talking with children about praying to invite Jesus into their life:

- <u>When possible, talk with children individually</u>. If you are telling stories to a large group of children that express the thought of inviting Jesus into their life, create an opportunity for each one to speak individually with you or another trained person. A child's personal relationship with Jesus Christ is dealt with most effectively one-on-one rather than in a group. Also, children talk more freely when they are away from group pressure.

- <u>Allow for free choice, and avoid pressure</u>. The love of God is offered to us individually. Creating ways for children to respond individually to God's love without pressure allows their response to be a genuine response to God, not one to please peers, parents, a teacher, or in response to a gift. On page 17 of *The Greatest Promise* booklet, there is a question asking the child if he or she wants to pray the prayer to invite Jesus into his or her life right now. This question is provided to give the child the opportunity to say yes or no as you are reading the question. If the child answers the question with "no," then stop. Leave the door open by saying something like, "Okay, that is fine. When you are ready to talk about this again, please come and talk with me."

Remember that children want to please the significant adults in their lives. Make sure your presentation is simple, clear, and allows response to the Holy Spirit and not to an adult personality.

- <u>Depend on the Holy Spirit for guidance</u>. If a child's decision to invite Jesus into his or her life is due to someone's pressure rather than the conviction of the Holy Spirit, confusion and doubt result. Ask the Holy Spirit for wisdom, and be confident that He will guide your conversation.

- <u>Be sure that the invitation for children to ask Jesus to live with them and in them is an intrinsic part of their character and spiritual formation.</u> Learning and knowing Bible stories, memorizing Bible verses, learning and singing songs about God and Jesus, and learning to talk and listen to God are essential. So is giving children the choice to ask Jesus to come and live in them. Just as we are careful that the decision is the child's, we want the child to know that he or she has the opportunity to make a voluntary choice.

Some years ago Moody Press published figures stating that 85 percent of all Christian conversions occur between the ages of four and fourteen.[4]

George Barna recently published research that reinforces this idea.[5] Based on a nationwide, representative sampling of more than 4,200 young people and adults, the survey data shows that adults ages nineteen to death have only a 6 percent probability of accepting Christ as their Savior. Young people ages fourteen through eighteen have just a 4 percent probability of doing so. However, children between the ages of five and thirteen have a 32 percent probability of making a voluntary choice to invite Jesus into their lives.

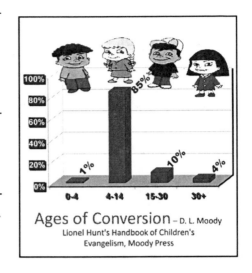

Ages of Conversion – D. L. Moody
Lionel Hunt's Handbook of Children's
Evangelism, Moody Press

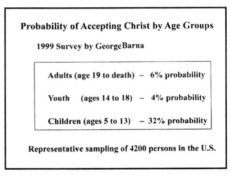

Probability of Accepting Christ by Age Groups

1999 Survey by George Barna

Adults (age 19 to death) – 6% probability

Youth   (ages 14 to 18) – 4% probability

Children (ages 5 to 13) – 32% probability

Representative sampling of 4200 persons in the U.S.

What do these statistics say to you? What about the other issues of guiding children to a personal relationship with Jesus that I have raised in this chapter? I am convinced that we can't begin too soon to develop the character and spiritual life of children toward God through His Son Jesus. Our task is to be wise about the ways children develop, think, and learn; model our faith in God; and demonstrate God's character in everyday, ordinary life. Children are able to take on God's character, follow God's ways, and develop an intimate relationship with God beyond what might be expected for their years.

"Teach me, O lord, to follow your decrees [ways]; then I will keep them to the end" (Psalm 119:33).

NOTES

[1] *Renovaré Regional Conference on Spiritual Renewal*, February 1–2, 2008, p. 22.
[2] Wes Haystead, *Teaching Your Child About God* (Ventura, CA: Regal Books GL Publication, 1983), 131.
[3] Vernie Schorr, 1990, The JESUS Film Project, reprinted by Foursquare Missions Press with permission.
[4] Lionel Hunt, *Handbook of Children's Evangelism* (Chicago: Moody Press, 1960)
[5] George Barna, "Evangelism Is Most Effective Among Kids" Barna Update (October 11, 2004).

Think on These Things

List some of the misunderstandings of God, Jesus, church, or other Christian concepts that you recall from your childhood.

_____

_____

_____

Practice It!

Keeping in mind the age-appropriate guidelines, the language, and the examples you have just read, evaluate and make note of the ways and materials you are using to:

Help build your children's life with God and His Son Jesus _____

_____

_____

_____

Prepare them to invite Jesus into their life _____

_____

_____

_____

APPENDIX

The Eight Foundation Virtues
Definitions and Benefits to Society

Compassion

Definition: Compassion is sympathy for someone else's suffering or misfortune, together with the desire to help, and appropriate action for his or her benefit.

Benefits to society: All people want and need compassion. When people build relationships on compassion rather than power, they act to give to each other the best they have. Compassion allows people to bear all things, believe all things, hope all things, and endure all things.

Scripture basis: "Jesus called his disciples to him and said, 'I have compassion for these people; they have already been with me three days and have nothing to eat. I do not want to send them away hungry, or they may collapse on the way'" (Matthew 15:32). In this Scripture, we see that Jesus lived out the private, inward compassion of His Father.

"[The Lord] crowns you with love and compassion" (Psalm 103:4).

Forgiveness

Definition: Forgiveness means to no longer blame or be angry with someone who has hurt or wronged you, including yourself. Forgiveness is to pardon or excuse a wrong thought, word, attitude, or action without condition.

Benefits to society: When people practice forgiveness in the community, they break the cycle of revenge. When a person experiences forgiveness, he or she is freed from guilt and attitudes of failure. When people feel they have failed, they lose their productivity. When people receive forgiveness, they regain their motivation to contribute to society.

Scripture basis: "Love your enemies, do good to them... and you will be sons of the Most High, because he is kind to the ungrateful and wicked" (Luke 6:35). Notice that this Scripture points to an intimate connection between compassion and forgiveness.

"If you forgive others their trespasses, your heavenly Father will also forgive you" (Matthew 6:14, NRSV).

"Bear with each other and forgive whatever grievances you may have against one another. Forgive as the Lord forgave you" (Colossians 3:13).

Integrity

Definition: Integrity is strength and firmness of character that results in consistent sincerity and honesty. People of integrity keep their word.

Benefits to society: Many systems of law and justice are based upon the Bible. These teachings provide an absolute standard for integrity so that society can determine whether the action of an individual is acceptable or not. An absolute standard keeps corrupt leaders from making one law for the people and another law for themselves. As people act with integrity, integrity is infused into society, bringing maximum value to the law.

Scripture basis: "In everything...show integrity, seriousness and soundness of speech" (Titus 2:7–8).

Respect

Definition: Respect is showing honor to people by listening, being courteous and polite, and demonstrating manners. It includes self-respect, the avoidance of excessive self-criticism, and respect for order and authority.

Benefits to society: People promote respect by considering others as important as themselves. Respect is an outcome of demonstrating honor to people. The result is a society that demonstrates respect for order and authority.

Scripture basis: "Each of you must respect his mother and father" (Leviticus 19:3a). "Rise in the presence of the aged, show respect for the elderly and revere your God. I am the lord" (Leviticus 19:32).

Responsibility

Definition: Responsibility is the personal, individual acceptance that every human being is accountable for his or her behavior, including thoughts, choices, decisions, speech, and actions.

Benefits to society: Individuals, families, and social groups win when each carries its share of responsibility. When a society is made up of responsible citizens, it is possible to focus on ways to solve problems through logical consequence, moral character, conscience, and right and wrong.

Scripture basis: "Each person must be responsible for himself" (Galatians 6:5b, ICB).

Initiative

Definition: Initiative is choosing to take the first step in thinking, doing, or learning. It includes being responsible for follow-through. Initiative is demonstrating responsible thoughts and actions without being prompted or without being influenced by limited choices.

Benefits to society: Initiative is grounded in first steps and follow-through. Initiative results in the ability to create, to solve problems, and to continue what is begun until it is completed. People who initiate are risk takers and are character driven. They act without prompting and take the first steps in resolving disputes. These behaviors, attitudes, and conduct result in a society of responsible citizens with positive, productive work ethics; constructive attitudes toward others; and motivation to provide solutions.

Scripture basis: "I can do all things through Christ because he gives me strength" (Philippians 4:13, ICB).

Cooperation

Definition: Cooperation is working together to reach a common goal. A cooperative person is willing to work with others in an effort to accomplish something that cannot be achieved by a single person. Cooperation is sharing skills, energy, talents, respect, and responsibility with others.

Benefits to society: The mutual good of society is more likely to be attained when people work, play, and study cooperatively. No one person is able to accomplish all that is needed for a society. By working together, people can strive collectively to educate their young, make medical care possible, maintain law and order, make housing and food available, provide products and services, and temper the worst aspects of competition.

Scripture basis: "Two people are better than one. They get more done by working together" (Ecclesiastes 4:9, ICB).

Perseverance

Definition: Perseverance is continual, steady effort made to fulfill some purpose, goal, task, or commitment. It means persistence in spite of difficulties, opposition, or discouragement. Perseverance is the refusal to give up when things are difficult. It is the habit of following through and finishing what was started.

Benefits to society: When individuals practice perseverance, they contribute to society the ability to see a task or commitment through to completion, and to keep doing right regardless of problems or persecution. The ability to persevere is foundational for education, employment, religion, relationships, leadership, and marriage.

Scripture basis: "The testing of your faith develops perseverance. Perseverance must finish its work so that you may be mature and complete, not lacking anything" (James 1:3-4).

Examples of Age-Appropriate Stories for Character Virtues

Following is a list of stories for use in teaching character virtues. They are organized by virtues. Within each group, they are further organized by age level. Note: Older books may be difficult to find, as publishers sometimes change and books are updated and re-released in various formats. Hard-to-find titles can be located at www.barnesandnoble.com.

Stories to Teach the Character Virtue of Compassion
Preschool and Kindergarten

Berenstain, Stan and Jan. *The Berenstain Bears Think of Those in Need.* New York: Random House, 1999.

Fox, Mem. *Wilfrid Gordon McDonald Partridge.* New York: Kane/Miller, 1985.

Joosse, Barbara M. *I Love You the Purplest.* San Francisco: Chronicle Books, 1996.

Joosse, Barbara M. *Mama, Do You Love Me?* San Francisco: Chronicle Books, 1991.

Heide, Florence Parry and Roxanne. *I Love Every-People.* St. Louis: Concordia Publishing House, 1978.

Lucado, Max. *The Crippled Lamb.* Nashville: Thomas Nelson, 1994.

McMullan, Kate. *If You Were My Bunny.* New York: Scholastic, Inc., 1996.

Wilhelm, Hans. *I'll Always Love You.* New York: Crown Publishers, 1985.

Grades 1–2

Caple, Kathy. *Harry's Smile.* New York: Houghton Mifflin Company, 1987.
   Picture book. 32 pages. Harry is hesitant to meet a pen pal for fear she won't like his looks. He finally realizes she likes him for who he is, not how he looks.

Carlson, Nancy. *I Like Me!* New York: Puffin Books, 1990.
   30 brightly colored pages. Formation of a healthy self image is the basis for a happy and useful life.

Deluis, Dom. *Charlie the Caterpillar.* New York: Simon & Schuster, 1993.

Picture book. 32 pages. Charlie has compassion on another caterpillar because he knows how it is to be rejected.

Flournoy, Valerie. *The Best Time of Day.* New York: Random House, 1978.

Fox, Mem. *Wilfrid Gordon McDonald Partridge.* New York: Kane/Miller, 1985.

Picture book. A boy lives next to an old people's home and befriends several people in an effort to help his favorite friend find her memory.

Goble, Paul. *Love Flute.* New York: Simon & Schuster, 1992.

Greenway, Jennifer. *A Real Little Bunny, A Sequel to the Velveteen Rabbit.* Kansas City, MO: Andrews & McMeel, 1993.

A lonely bunny learns that with love, all things are possible.

Joosse, Barbara M. *Mama, Do You Love Me?* San Francisco: Chronicle Books, 1991.

This book is also listed under the Preschool and Kindergarten section but is appropriate for young first graders as well.

Martin, Bill, Jr. *Knots on a Counting Rope.* New York: Henry Holt and Co., 1966.

Munsch, Robert. *Love You Forever.* Ontario, Canada: Firefly Books Ltd., 1986.

Polacco, Patricia. *Mrs. Katz and Tush.* New York: Bantam Doubleday Dell, 1992.

Schenk de Regniers, Beatrice. *Everyone Is Good for Something.* New York: Clarion Books, 1980.

26 pages. A folk tale about a boy whose compassion for a cat leads to the development of his own self-esteem and success.

Schneider, Richard. *Why Christmas Trees Aren't Perfect.* Nashville: Abingdon Press, 2007.

Picture book. A Christmas story about a tree that shows love, kindness, and gentleness to animals and birds in the forest.

Silverstein, Shel. *The Giving Tree.* New York: HarperCollins, 1964.

Waber, Bernard. *You Look Ridiculous, Said the Rhinoceros to the Hippopotamus.* New York: Houghton Mifflin, 1966.

Picture book. A young hippo learns to be content with himself.

Williams, Margery. *The Velveteen Rabbit.* New York: Simon & Schuster, 1983.

The tale of a neglected toy who dreams of becoming real and a little boy whose love makes that dream come true.

Grades 3–4

Cohen, Barbara. *Molly's Pilgrim.* New York: Lothrop, Lee & Shephard, 1983.

Molly's Jewish mother helps her dress a pilgrim doll for a Thanksgiving play. Could also be used for courage and perseverance. Literature unit available from Teacher Created Materials. In video form as well.

Johnson, Jan. *Brother Francis.* Minneapolis, MN: Winston Press, 1977.

A story about Saint Francis of Assisi.

MacLachlan, Patricia. *Sarah, Plain and Tall.* New York: HarperCollins, 1985.

58 pages. A tender story about the fragile beginnings of a family relationship when a woman from Maine comes to the frontier to help a widower with two small children keep his family together. Newberry Award Winner.

Williams, Margery. *The Velveteen Rabbit.* New York: Simon & Schuster, 1983.

This book is also listed under Grades 1–2 but is appropriate for young third graders as well.

Grade 5

Cleary, Beverly. *Dear Mr. Henshaw.* New York: HarperCollins, 1983.

A boy expresses his feelings to a teacher about the divorce of his parents.

O'Brien, Robert C. *Mr. Frisby and the Rats of Nimh.* New York: Simon & Schuster, 1971.

Smith, Doris Buchanan. *A Taste of Blackberries.* New York: HarperCollins, 1973.

Deals with the death of a friend.

Stories to Teach the Character Virtue of Forgiveness
Preschool and Kindergarten

Berenstain, Stan and Jan.
Berenstain Bears Get in a Fight. New York: Random House, 1982.
Berenstain Bears and the Bully. New York: Random House, 1993.
Berenstain Bears and Too Much Teasing. New York: Random House, 1995.
Cosby, Bill. *Meanest Thing to Say,* Little Bill Books for Beginning Readers. New York: Scholastic: 1997.
Duncan, Riana. *When Emily Woke Up Angry.* New York: Barrons Educational Series, 1989.
Keane, Glen. *Adam Raccoon and the Circus Master.* Colorado Springs, CO: David C. Cook, l989.
Mayer, Mercer. *I Was So Mad.* New York: Random House, 2000.
Nichols, Roy and Doris. *I'm No Ordinary Chicken* (Young Friends Series). Worthy Pub, 1987.
Richardson, John. *Bad Mood Bear.* New York: Barrons Educational Series, 1988.
Simon, Norma. *I Was So Mad!* Morton Grove, IL: Albert Whitman & Company, 1974.
Viorst, Judith. *I'll Fix Anthony.* New York: Simon & Schuster, 1988.

Grades 1–2

Levitin, Sonia. *The Man Who Kept His Heart in a Bucket.* New York: Penguin, 1991.
Picture book. 32 pages. Jack learns the secrets of his heart and finds joy again. Good use of symbolism and riddles.
Nichols, Roy and Doris. *I'm No Ordinary Chicken* (Young Friends Series). Worthy Pub, 1987.
Hattie asks forgiveness for the way she treated her friends when she is treated the same way by some strange chickens.
Viorst, Judith. *I'll Fix Anthony.* New York: Simon & Schuster, 1988.

A six-year-old boy seeks revenge on his mean older brother. Revenge is the opposite of forgiveness.

Grades 3–4

Cleary, Beverly. *Ellen Tebbitts.* New York: HarperCollins, 1990.
160 pages. Ellen experiences a restored relationship with a friend through forgiveness.

Yolen, Jane. *Letting Swift River Go.* Boston, MA: Little, Brown & Co., 1995.
Picture book with a deeper meaning. True story of how Sara Jane learns to let go of her attitudes of unfairness when her town was flooded to make a reservoir for Boston.

Grade 5

Alcott, Louisa May. *Little Women.* New York: Penguin, 1983.
Chapter 7: Jo must learn to forgive her sister Amy when she burns her manuscript.

Bunting, Eve. *The In-Between Days.* New York: HarperCollins, 1994.
119 pages. George faces some difficult consequences of his actions and must seek forgiveness for his family to become whole. Repentance as an aspect of forgiveness is discussed.

Byars, Betsy. *The Summer of the Swans.* New York: Viking Penguin, 1970.
142 pages. Sara learns to forgive and break the cycle of revenge when she trusts a friend to help her find her lost handicapped brother.

Yates, Elizabeth. *Amos Fortune: Free Man.* New York: Penguin, 1950.
181 pages. Amos has an opportunity to forgive white people who mistreat him and others.

Stories to Teach the Character Virtue of Integrity
Preschool and Kindergarten

Berenstain, Stan and Jan. *The Berenstain Bears and the Truth.* New York: Random House, 1983.

Cosby, Bill. *My Big Lie.* New York: Scholastic, 1999.

Little Red Riding Hood. (Traditional story available from multiple publishers.)

The Gingerbread Boy. (Traditional story available from multiple publishers.)

<u>*Grades 1–2*</u>

Aardema, Verna. *Pedro and the Padre: A Tale from Jalisco, Mexico.* New York: Dial Books for Young Readers, 1991.

Anderson, Hans Christian. *The Emperor's New Clothes.* Little, Brown & Co., 1984.

Berenstain, Stan and Jan. *The Berenstain Bears and the Truth.* New York: Random House, 1983.

dePaola, Tomie. "The Shepherd Who Cried Wolf" by Aesop, as retold by Tomie dePaola in *Tomie dePaola's Favorite Nursery Tales.* New York: Penguin, 1986.

Demi, Hitz. *Chen Ping and His Magic Axe.* New York: Penguin, 1987.

Pfister, Marcus. *The Rainbow Fish.* New York: North-South Books, 1992.

A wise octopus gives the Rainbow Fish advice on how to be liked.

Waber, Bernard. *Ira Sleeps Over.* Boston: Houghton Miffin, 1972.

<u>*Grades 3–4*</u>

Fleischman, Sid. *The Whipping Boy.* New York: HarperCollins, 1986.

Sharmat, Marjorie Weinman. *Gladys Told Me to Meet Her Here.* New York: HarperCollins, 1970.

Smith, Doris Buchanan. *A Taste of Blackberries.* New York: HarperCollins, 1973.

85 pages. The friendship between two boys is interrupted by death, leaving many questions to be face.

White, E.B. *Charlotte's Web.* New York: HarperCollins, 1952.

<u>*Grade 5*</u>

Bauer, Marion. *On My Honor.* New York: Bantam Doubleday Dell, 1986.

90 pages. A gripping portrayal of a boy's struggle with his conscience.

Brink, Carol R. *Caddie Woodlawn*. New York: Simon & Schuster, 1997.

Stories to Teach the Character Virtue of Respect
Preschool and Kindergarten

Berenstain, Stan and Jan. *The Berenstain Bears Forget Their Manners.*
New York: Random House, 1985.
Mama Bear comes up with a plan to correct the Bear family's rude
behavior.

Bridwell, Norman. *Clifford's Manners*. New York: Scholastic, 1987.

Cherry, Lynne. *The Great Kapok Tree: A Tale of the Amazon Rain Forest.*
New York: Harcourt, 1990.

Hallinan, P.K. *A Rainbow of Friends*. Nashville, TN: Ideals
Publications, 1995.
A story in verse about how all friends are special and valuable re-
gardless of differences or difficulties.

Keller, Irene, and Dick Keller. *The Thingumajig Book of Manners.*
Nashville, TN: Ideals Publications, 1999.

Cheltenham Elementary School Kindergarten. *We Are All Alike, We
Are All Different*. New York: Scholastic, 2003.

West, Colin. *Pardon? Said the Giraffe*. New York: HarperCollins, 1986.

McBratney, Sam. *Guess How Much I Love You*. Cambridge, MA:
Candlewick Press, 1994.

Waite, Michael. *Sir Maggie the Mighty: A Book about Obedience*. Colorado
Springs, CO: David C. Cook, 1989.

Grades 1–2

Aliki. *Manners*. New York: HarperCollins, 1991.

Allard, Harry.
Miss Nelson Is Missing. New York: Houghton Mifflin, 1985.
Miss Nelson Is Back. New York: Houghton Mifflin, 1986.
Miss Nelson Has a Field Day. New York: Houghton Mifflin, 1988.
Children in Room 207 learn obedience and courtesy when Viola
Swamp comes to substitute.

Brett, Jan. *Annie and the Wild Animals.* New York: Houghton Mifflin, 1985.
Annie shows patience and tolerance when her cat leaves during the winter, and she tries to develop friendships with wild animals.

Bunting, Eve.
The Mother's Day Mice. New York: Houghton Mifflin, 1986.
Three little mice set out to honor their mother on Mother's Day.
The Wednesday Surprise. New York: Houghton Mifflin, 1989.
A girl helps her grandmother learn to read and surprises the entire family.

Carle, Eric. *The Mixed-Up Chameleon.* New York: HarperCollins, 1988.

Frasier, Debra. *On the Day You Were Born.* New York: Harcourt, 1991.
Respect for each individual on the planet is encouraged. Wonderful birthday book.

Peet, Bill. *The Wump World.* New York: Houghton Mifflin, 1970.

Grades 3–4

Buscaglia, Leo. *A Memory for Tino.* New York: HarperCollins, 1988.
50 pages. A young boy shows respect for the elderly and gains a friend.

Mathis, Sharon Bell. *The Hundred Penny Box.* New York: Penguin, 2006.
A story of respect that a young boy experiences for his elderly great-great aunt.

Grade 5

Lewis, C. S. *The Lion, the Witch and the Wardrobe.* New York: Harper Collins, 1950.
Great literature for children dealing with many character qualities.

Polocco, Patricia. *The Keeping Quilt.* New York: Simon & Schuster, 1998.

Stories to Teach the Character Virtue of Responsibility
Preschool and Kindergarten

Bender, Marie. *Responsibility Counts.* Edina, MN: Abdo Publishing Co., 2003.

Doudna, Kelly. *Right On Time*. Edina, MN: Abdo Publishing Co., 2007.

Kenney, Cindy and Doug Peterson. *The Snooze Brothers*. Grand Rapids: Zondervan, 2006.

A lesson in responsibility.

Meiners, Cheri J. *Be Careful and Stay Safe*. Minneapolis, MN: Free Spirit Publishing, Inc., 2007.

Wilson, Karma. *I Will Rejoice: Celebrating Psalm 118*. Grand Rapids: Zonderkidz, 2000.

Based on Psalm 118:24, this story encourages children to be responsible by choosing to be joyful in everyday life activities.

Grades 1–2

Bunting, Eve. *Fly Away Home*. New York: Houghton Mifflin, 1991.

A sensitive look at homelessness and meeting life's challenges.

Griffith, Helen. *Georgia Music*. New York: HarperCollins, 1990.

A young girl and her mother take care of the grandfather when he is too old to live alone.

Grades 3–4

Bulla, Clyde R. *Shoeshine Girl*. New York: HarperCollins, 1975.

84 pages. Sara's bad attitude is changed by her association with Al, the owner of a shoeshine stand, as she learns the joy of acting with responsibility.

Shaw, Janet. *Kirsten Learns a Lesson*. Middleton, WI: American Girl Publishing, 1986.

61 pages. Kirsten shows consideration and responsibility when she makes the decision to stay with her family rather than go with her Indian friend.

Grade 5

Frank, Ann, *Diary of a Young Girl*. New York: Bantam Books, 1952.

A Jewish girl during WW II demonstrates discipline and self-control.

Lawson, Robert. *Ben and Me: An Astonishing Life of Benjamin Franklin by His Good Mouse Amos*. New York: Little, Brown & Company, 1988.

Paterson, Katherine.
> *The Great Gilly Hopkins.* New York: HarperCollins, 1978.
> *The Bridge to Terebithia.* New York: HarperCollins, 1977.
Speare, Elizabeth. *The Bronze Bow.* New York: Houghton Mifflin, 1961.

Stories to Teach the Character Virtue of Initiative
Preschool and Kindergarten

Klingel, Cynthia.
> *Friendliness.* Mankato, MN: The Child's World, 2008.
> *Generosity.* Mankato, MN: The Child's World, 2008.
Meiners, Cheri. *Talk and Work It Out.* Minneapolis, MN: Free Spirit Publishing Inc., 2005.
Schuette, Sarah. *I Am A Leader.* Mankato, MN: Capstone Press, 2007.

Grades 1–2

Bunting, Eve. *St. Patrick's Day In the Morning.* New York: Houghton Mifflin, 1980.
> Jamie takes the initiative to prove to himself that he is capable of being in the St. Patrick's Day parade.
Marzollo, Jean. *In 1776.* New York: Scholastic, 1994.
> Picture book. The initiative and courage of the colonists is told in rhyme for very young children.
O'Nan, Lawrence W. and Gerald D. *The Adventures of Andy Ant Series.* Wheaton, IL: Tyndale House Publishers, 1988.

Grades 2–4

> *Lawn Mower on the Loose*
> *Runaway Ant*
> *The Band-Music Mystery*
> *The Swimming Hole Disaster*
Rosen, Michael. *We're Going on a Bear Hunt.* New York: Simon & Schuster, 1989.
> Four children and their father make a valiant effort at courage and boldness in going on a bear hunt.

Speare, Elizabeth. *Somebody Loves You, Mr. Hatch.* New York: Simon & Schuster, 1992.

Mr. Hatch finds courage and motivation when he believes someone loves him. Also self-esteem.

Grades 3–4

Hoffman, Mary. *Amazing Grace.* New York: Dial, 1991.

A story of an African American girl who is encouraged to be all she can be.

Speare, Elizabeth. *The Sign of the Beaver.* New York: Houghton Mifflin, 1983.

Left alone in the wilderness while his father returns for the family, Matt teaches a young Indian boy to read, and together they survive the fierce winter.

Speare, Elizabeth. *Somebody Loves You, Mr. Hatch.* New York: Simon & Schuster, 1992.

Mr. Hatch finds courage and motivation when he believes someone loves him. Also self-esteem.

Grade 5

Dickens, Monica. *The Great Fire.* New York: Doubleday, 1970.

A twelve-year-old boy, Peter, demonstrates courage in the London fire.

Lowry, Lois. *Number the Stars.* New York: Bantam Doubleday Dell, 1989.

Two girls in Denmark encounter a situation during World War II in which courage is necessary.

Yashima, Taro. *Crow Boy.* New York: Penguin Books, 1977.

Stories to Teach the Character Virtue of Cooperation
Preschool and Kindergarten

Donahue, Jill. *Being Cooperative.* Minneapolis: Picture Windows Books, 2008.

King, Alyson. *Chores Around the House.* Vero Beach, FL: Rourke Publishing, 2007.

Mattern, Joanne. *Do You Take Turns?* New York: Gareth Stevens, Inc., 2007.

Meiners, Cheri. *Join In and Play.* Minneapolis, MN: Free Spirit Publishing, 2004.

Grades 1–2

Bunting, Eve. *The Valentine Bears.* New York: Houghton Mifflin, 2004.
Picture book. Humorous story of valentine kindness between two hibernating bears.

Heine, Helme. *Friends.* New York: Simon & Schuster, 1982.
A lighthearted story of how three friends make it through life as they work together.

Henkes, Kevin. *Julius, the Baby of the World.* New York: Harper Collins, 1990.
Older sister Lilly learns to replace jealousy with cooperation when a new baby arrives.

Grades 3–4

Herriot, James. *The Market Square Dog.* New York: St. Martin's Press, 1989.
A village cooperates in the care of a stray dog who finally finds a home.

Wilder, Laura Ingalls. *Little House Series,* New York: Harper & Row, 1932.
Life on the early American frontier is depicted with many character traits portrayed by the Ingalls family and other characters in the books.

Grade 5

Dahl, Roald. *Charlie and the Chocolate Factory.* New York: Penguin, 1964.
Charlie and his elderly grandparents cooperate in winning a prize. Many negative character qualities are displayed by other children.

L'Engle, Madeline.
A Wrinkle in Time. New York: Square Fish, 1962.

The Arm of the Starfish. New York: Random House, 1965.

Stories to Teach the Character Virtue of Perseverance
Preschool and Kindergarten

Andrews-Goebel. *The Pot That Juan Built.* New York: Low Books, 2002.

Kenney, Cindy, and Doug Peterson. *Frog Wars.* Grand Rapids: Zonderkidz, 2005.
A lesson in perseverance.

Klingel, Cynthia. *Loyalty.* Mankato, MN: The Child's World, 2008.

Meiners, Cheri. *Try and Stick With It.* Minneapolis, MN: Free Spirit Publishing, 2004.

Grades 1–2

Brown, Margaret Wise. *The Runaway Bunny.* New York: Harper Collins, 1942.
A little bunny keeps running away from his mother in an imaginative and imaginary game of verbal hide-and-seek. Children will be profoundly comforted by this lovingly steadfast mother who finds her child every time.

Bunting, Eve. *Sunflower House.* New York: Harcourt Brace, 1996.
Picture book. A young boy creates a summer playhouse by planting sunflowers and saves the seeds to make another house the next year.

Clements, Andrew. *Big Al.* New York: Simon & Schuster, 1988.
Picture book, 30 pages. A fish demonstrates perseverance in developing friendships.

Diestel-Feddersen, Mary. *Try Again, Sally Jane.* Milwaukee, WI: Gareth Stevens, 1987.
Picture book. 30 pages. Sally Jane's animal friends encourage her to keep trying to skate with her new roller skates.

Green, Phyllis. *The Fastest Quitter in Town.* Reading, MA: Addison-Wesley, 1972.

62 pages. Johnny earns the reputation of being a quitter, but through his love for his great-grandfather, he learns the importance of staying with a task.

Grades 3–4

Armstrong, Jennifer. *Black-eyed Susan.* New York: Random House, 1995.
120 pages. Susie, age 10, sees her father struggle to establish a homestead and her mother struggle to overcome her loneliness and isolation.

Naylor, Phyllis. *Shiloh.* New York: Simon & Schuster, 2000.
141 pages. Marty shows great perseverance and courage in trying to protect the dog he loves from an owner he suspects is mistreating him.

Tripp, Valerie. *Felicity Learns a Lesson.* Middleton, WI: Pleasant Company, 1991.
69 pages. Felicity faces the problem of how to be loyal to her father and to her friend.

Grade 5

Armstrong, William. *Sounder.* New York: Harper Collins, 1972.
116 pages. A boy refuses to give up the search for his father after his father has been arrested.

Hemingway, Ernest. *The Old Man and the Sea.* New York: Simon & Schuster, 1952.
The story of a Cuban fisherman's relentless, agonizing battle with a giant marlin.

Henry, Marguerite. *Misty of Chincoteague.* New York: Simon & Schuster, 1947.
173 pages. Paul and Maureen are determined to catch a wild horse and win the town race.

McGovern, Ann. *Runaway Slave.* New York: Scholastic Book Services, 1967.
The story of Harriet Tubman.

Viorst, Judith. *Alexander and the Terrible, Horrible, No Good, Very Bad Day.* New York: Macmillan Publishing, 1972.

Other Sources

Schorr, Vernie. *The Greatest Promise.* Orlando, FL: The JESUS Film Project, 1990.

The Greatest Promise booklet has pictures and a brief clear story of God's promise to make a way to live with Him forever. For very young children, you may choose some of the pictures to look at and talk about. The booklet may be read over and over, guiding and building a child's attitude and understanding of God's promises. Copies available through Character Choice. www.characterchoice. org.

The Story of Jesus, DVD video (The JESUS Film Project, P.O. Box 620546, Orlando, FL 32862, 800-432-1997), available in 129 languages.

This is the story of Jesus as seen through the eyes of children who might have lived during the time Jesus lived on earth. Follow the lives of Benjamin, Caleb, Sarah, Joel, Leah, and Nathan living in Jerusalem about AD 32. Children of all ages will enjoy this captivating retelling of the true story of Jesus from a child's perspective. Available through www.jesusforchildren.org.

Example of Preschool-Kindergarten Compassion Session Titled "The Man Who Helped"

This partial session (reproduced on the pages that follow) demonstrates a compassion song, a readiness activity, a compassion story, questions to talk about after the story, and one practice and application activity. The full session appears in the "Character Formation" curriculum available through Character Choice (www.characterchoice.org). The curriculum includes all of the above plus a puppet script, a transition rhyme, a finger play, another compassion song, activity pages, and a worship and prayer time.

Example of Elementary Integrity Session Titled "An Honest Thinker"

Following the example compassion session pages is a partial session on integrity that demonstrates a readiness activity, an integrity story, questions to talk about after the story, and two practice and apply activities. The full session appears in the "Character Formation" curriculum available through Character Choice (www.characterchoice.org). The curriculum includes all of the above plus three more practice and apply activities, an integrity creed, and activity pages.

MODULE 1: COMPASSION
SESSION 3: The Man Who Helped

THE MAN WHO HELPED

Definition
Compassion is sympathy for someone else's suffering or misfortune, together with the desire to help.

Words to Live By
When we help people, we show people God's love.

Benefits to Society
When people build relationships on compassion rather then power, they are able to give to each other the best they have. All people want and need compassion. Compassion allows people to bear all things, believe all things, hope all things, and endure all things.

Main Christian Principle/Concept
Jesus has compassion for all people. Compassion is caring, giving comfort, and demonstrating kindness and empathy to friends and people who are different from us.

Key Bible Verse
"Show mercy to others; be kind, humble, gentle and patient."
Colossians 3:12

Focus (Session Goals)
Each child may discover that just as Jesus took time to love and care for all people, we are to love and care for people too. Learners may identify ways to love and care for people and practice loving and caring for people in the classroom, at home, and in the neighborhood.

MODULE 1: COMPASSION   **CHARACTER FORMATION**
SESSION 3: The Man Who Helped   **Preschool-Kindergarten**

 Preparation/Materials Needed for the Session: Read Luke 10:25-37. Read the story "The Man Who Helped" to enable you to tell it in your own words. Have the Carrie Compassion puppet ready to help you with the Readiness Activity: Review/Focus and to tell the story; activity pages for each learner; materials needed for the activities you choose.

 Note to Teacher: As you gather the children, sing the character song "Compassion."

SONG — "Compassion"
(Tune: "Mary Had a Little Lamb")

Have compassion, learn to care,
Learn to share, everywhere.
Have compassion, help someone,
God's love and work is done.

Have compassion, give your best,
Nothing less, just say, "Yes!"
Have compassion, help someone,
Then God's love and work is done.

READINESS ACTIVITY: Review/Focus

 Guided Conversation:

Who is the special friend who has been helping us learn to be Compassion Givers? **[Allow children to answer that it is Carrie Compassion.]** I wonder where she is? Maybe if we call her name, she will join us. **[Allow children to call her.]**

MODULE 1: COMPASSION   **CHARACTER FORMATION**
SESSION 3: The Man Who Helped   **Preschool-Kindergarten**

Carrie Compassion says: Hi everyone! It's so nice to see you again! Thank you for caring about me and calling me to come and be with you. You are becoming Compassion Givers!

Remember, **compassion** is a word that means caring for someone else—to be kind to someone who is sad or hurting, or to show someone that we love them by doing kind things or by keeping promises. We're going to learn more about **compassion** today.

Do you remember in our last story that we talked about ways Jesus showed us God's love? He did this by doing very special things. What were some of these special things? **[Answers: Helped blind people see; helped people who couldn't walk to walk again; made sick people well; provided food for people when they were hungry.]**

Carrie Compassion: What is one word for these kinds of special things? **[Answer: Miracles— something only Jesus and God can do.]**

How did Jesus help Jairus' little girl? **[Answer: She died and He made her alive and well again.]**

Why did Jesus heal and help people? **[Answer: To show people God loves and cares for them.]** Please say these words with me. **[Repeat "to show people God loves and cares for them" with the children.]**

Let's get ready to listen to a new story I have to tell you today. It is a story Jesus told to help people learn to care for others. It is a story about a very kind man who helped a man he did not know. You have a part in telling the story. When I say, *"Someone is coming,"* please say, *"Step, step, step,"* and pat your legs very quietly, one hand at a time. **[Practice this with the children several times.]**

When you hear talk about a donkey, please say, *"Clip-clop, clip-clop,"* and pat your legs one hand at a time, this time a little louder. **[Practice several times with the children.]**

Place your hands in your lap when you ready to start. **[Pause.]** Now listen carefully so you will know when it is your turn to help tell the story.

STORY TIME

"The Man Who Helped"
a preschool/kindergarten level Bible story
from Luke 10:25-37

[Read or tell the story "The Man Who Helped." You are encouraged to share the story in your own words.]

One day a man was walking down a road all by himself. Some robbers saw him coming. They knocked him down. They took his money. Then they ran away. The man was hurt too badly to get up. He needed help! Who would help him?

Listen! Do you hear that <u>someone is coming</u>? **[Lead the children in saying "step, step, step" while patting their legs.]**

<u>Someone is coming</u> down the road—**STEP, STEP, STEP.** He is a very busy man with a very important job. Do you think he will help?

No! He saw the hurt man, but he didn't stop— **STEP, STEP, STEP.** He didn't care; he walked right by him.

Listen! Do you hear again that <u>someone is coming</u> down the road? **[Lead the children in saying "step, step, step" while patting their legs.]**

STEP, STEP, STEP. Do you think he will stop to help?

STEP, STEP, STEP. No! He went over and looked at the hurt man, and then he walked by on the other side of the road—**STEP, STEP, STEP.**

Listen! Do you hear a donkey coming down the road? **[Lead the children in saying "clip-clop, clip-clop."]**

MODULE 1: COMPASSION   **CHARACTER FORMATION**
SESSION 3: The Man Who Helped   **Preschool-Kindergarten**

A man on his donkey is coming down the road—**CLIP-CLOP, CLIP-CLOP!** Do you think he will help?—**CLIP-CLOP, CLIP-CLOP!**

YES! The man on the donkey stopped when he saw the hurt man—**CLIP-CLOP, CLIP-CLOP.** He helped the man. He put medicine on the man's hurt places. He put the hurt man on his donkey. He took the man with him. **CLIP-CLOP, CLIP-CLOP.**

He took the man to an inn—like a hotel or motel—and put him to bed. The hurt man slept all night. [**Put your hands together on the side of your head and lean your head to the side, as if you are sleeping. Encourage the children to make this motion too.**]

The next day he talked to the inn keeper, the man who took care of the inn, or hotel where they stayed. He said, "I must leave. Here is some money. Please take care of my new friend until he is well." The man got on his donkey and rode away. **CLIP-CLOP, CLIP-CLOP.**

Which one of the three men was the Compassion Giver? The first man who walked by? [**No.**] The second man who looked at the hurt man but walked by on the other side of the road? [**No.**] The third man who stopped and cared for the hurt man, took him to the hotel inn, and made sure he would be cared for until he was well? [**Yes.**]

 # TALK ABOUT IT

(Questions to talk about with learners after the story, with possible answers in brackets)

1. **What happened to the man who was walking down the road all by himself?** [Some robbers knocked him down and hurt him.]

2. **When the first man walked by the hurt man, what did he do?** [He walked right past; he didn't help the hurt man.]

3. **What did the second man do?** [He looked at the hurt man but walked by on the other side of the road.]

MODULE 1: COMPASSION   CHARACTER FORMATION
SESSION 3: The Man Who Helped   Preschool-Kindergarten

4. Who stopped to help the hurt man? [The man on the donkey.]

5. What did the man on the donkey do to show the hurt man compassion? [Possible answers: He put medicine on the hurt places; he took the hurt man to an inn and put him to bed; he gave the man who took care of the inn some money to care for the hurt man.)\]

6. How can you be a Compassion Giver and care for each other, for your family, and for your neighbors? [Listen to the children and help them think of ways they can be helpers at school, at home, and in their neighborhood.]

> When we help people who are hurting or are sad,
> we show people God's love. We show compassion!

 Note to Teacher: Following the telling of the story, assign parts as suggested. Encourage each child to dress in a Bible time costume.

 Guided Conversation:

Today's story is a wonderful story to act out or role play! Everyone will have a part in the story. Each of you may dress in a Bible time costume.

What kind of clothes did the people in Bible time wear? Here are some robes that look like what people wore in Bible times.

We can practice being compassion givers by helping one another choose and put on a costume.

Now it is time for you to act out the story. Who was in our story today? [As the children remember the people in the story, assign the parts to the children.

People: Man who is hurt
           First man who walks down the road
           Second man who walks down the road
           Man on donkey
           Inn keeper (hotel keeper)

MODULE 1: COMPASSION   **CHARACTER FORMATION**
SESSION 3: The Man Who Helped   **Preschool-Kindergarten**

The donkey (have ear patterns and donkey tail ready)

Create parts for all the children. You can have groups of children walk past the hurt man. Have all the children speak when it is time to say "STEP, STEP, STEP" or "CLIP-CLOP, CLIP-CLOP."]

Ready? Let's begin. **[Help the children act out the story as you retell it. At the end of each role play, ask the children: "How can we help people?" Doing this role play activity several times will allow the children to take turns playing these parts.]**

Activity Time — Make a Puzzle

Preparation/Materials Needed: A copy of Activity Page 1 for each child; felt markers and crayons. Give each child a copy of Activity Page 1. The Bible verse is on the activity page: "God is love...We love because God first loved us." 1 John 4:16, 19.

Guided Conversation:
Please enjoy coloring your picture. Take your time and think about ways you can be kind and caring and helpful, like the man with the donkey. **[Allow time for the children to complete their coloring.]**

When you have finished coloring, cut on the lines to create puzzle pieces. Then fit the pieces so that your picture is together again.

AN HONEST THINKER

Definition

Integrity is the strength and firmness of character that results in consistent sincerity and honesty. People of integrity keep their word.

Words to Live By

"Before you speak, ask yourself: Is it true? Is it kind? Is it necessary? If not, let it go unsaid."

An Old Saying

Benefits to Society

Society is influenced by the choices and ideas of the people who live within it. Truth, discernment, and integrity equip and enable people to make constructive choices. These choices are linked to ideologies that result in honest laws, absolute standards for behavior, and consequences that benefit society.

Main Christian Principle/Concept

Choices and ideas lead to more choices and ideas. Everything we think, everything we say, everything we do—all have consequences. Integrity requires honest thinking.

Key Bible Verse

Titus 2:8a
"And when you speak, speak the truth so you cannot be criticized."

Focus (Session Goals)

To introduce the concept honesty is crucial to being a person of integrity. To define the words *outcome* and *repercussion*. To guide children to identify everyday choices and the logical consequences of those choices. To give the opportunity for children to list ways they can be an "honest thinker."

MODULE 3: INTEGRITY
SESSION 15: An Honest Thinker

CHARACTER FORMATION
Grades 1 - 5

READINESS ACTIVITY

 Preparation/Materials Needed for this Session: Copy the Integrity Creed cards on stiff paper; cut the cards apart, making one for each learner. (See the Teacher Resource Page after the Summary.) Read the story, "An Honest Thinker." Chalkboard or poster paper; copies of Student Activity Pages, one for each learner.

 Note to Teacher: Gather the technology and materials needed for the "Define Words" activity.

 Guided Conversation:

In our last discussion, we determined that we live in a world where truth and lies are both part of life. If this statement is true, what do we continually need to think about in our everyday lives? [Answer: What is true and what is false.]

What are some other ideas we discussed about truth? [Possible answers: Truth is powerful. Truth brings control and security. Truth can be discerned by thinking critically.]

Truthfulness and honesty are two parts of integrity. Integrity starts with being truthful and honest. Here is an "Integrity Creed" for each of us to learn and memorize. [Give each learner an Integrity Creed card you have prepared from the Teacher Resource Page.]

> **INTEGRITY CREED**
>
> People can count on me because
> I am a person of integrity.
> I will do a little each day to help create
> a world that is more honest.
> When I make a mistake, I will be
> honest and accept the consequences of my choice.
> I am a person of integrity.
> You can count on me!

MODULE 3: INTEGRITY   **CHARACTER FORMATION**
SESSION 15: An Honest Thinker   **Grades 1 - 5**

As we are becoming people of integrity, we must be people who think and discern critically. Remember, to discern means to recognize something for what it is—right or wrong, true or false." Discerning and thinking critically make it possible for us to be honest and to make wise and constructive choices.

Choices and ideas always lead to more choices and ideas. Everything we think, everything we say, everything we do—all have consequences.

Think of some consequences you experience from your ideas or everyday choices.

[Allow children to respond. List their responses on the chalkboard or poster paper.]

Some possible responses:

> What we eat – *Meals and snacks affect our energy, our size, and our intellect.*

> What we say – *Words create positive attitudes and actions or are hurtful and destructive.*

> What we choose to do with our time – taking risks; sitting around and doing nothing; getting involved in too many activities

> Television viewing – *There are over 100 cable channels, violent shows; current events/news; educational programs.*

> Become depressed or experiencing joy. *We can choose to focus on ways to experience positive attitudes and actions.*

> How we dress – for school, work, play, sports, and church. *What is the logical consequence if dress is not appropriate?*]

Every choice we make, every idea and decision, leads to another choice, idea, or decision. Either we acknowledge this truth or deny it as reality.

Who we are now is the sum total of our choices, ideas, and decisions.

We have the opportunity to continue in a constructive direction or to choose a destructive direction.

MODULE 3: INTEGRITY **CHARACTER FORMATION**
SESSION 15: An Honest Thinker **Grades 1 - 5**

STORY TIME

"An Honest Thinker"
An elementary level story

In our story today, we are going to meet a young man named Zack Hollister, who rode for the Pony Express. Who knows what the Pony Express was? [Answer: It was a mail delivery service on horseback when the western part of the United States was being settled.]

The other person in this story besides Zack is a man who learned to live and travel alone in the high desert for eight years. His name is Hawk Tumball.

These two meet when Zack falls into a ravine while running from the Paiute Indians. He breaks both legs in the fall. Hawk finds him and nurses him back to health.

Hawk is somewhat of a hermit with a hermit's philosophy. He and Zack get into some very interesting conversations. In this chapter from the book *Grayfox*,[1] Hawk is talking to Zack about choices and ideas. Zack is telling the story. It begins with Hawk speaking.

"Everything you think, everything you do—it all has consequences. One idea or choice always leads to another, and another after that . . . and another after that. Just like heading that direction will lead to the Rockies, then to the Atlantic, and eventually around the world."

I didn't reply. I wanted to hear what he'd say next.

"If you say or do something, then what follows from it? I don't mean just down the road a little ways, but if you follow it all the way, clear to the end . . . all the way around the world? You get me, Zack?"

"I'm not sure."

"Every idea always leads to something else. Every choice you make moves you one step closer to something else. Every idea and choice has implications. They're like footprints. They line up in a direction, and that's the direction you're going in. Lotta folks never think of outcomes and repercussions. But me, I'm *always* trying to think of them. I'm uncomfortable and nervous if I'm not two or three steps ahead of myself."

"I've noticed that," I said. "Your eyes are always roving around, peering about, looking down the trail, up the mountain, ahead of us, behind us—all over."

Hawk laughed.

---

[1]This story is Chapter 24, "Cooking Up a Character Stew," from *Grayfox* by Michael Phillips, copyright 1993. Used with permission of Bethany House Publishers.

MODULE 3: INTEGRITY   **CHARACTER FORMATION**
SESSION 15: An Honest Thinker   **Grades 1 - 5**

"I don't suppose I even notice anymore," he said.

"You do it every second."

"I reckon you're right," he said. "Mostly I'm trying to keep a few steps ahead of myself in my thoughts and my choices. If I say something or do something, I want to know what it's likely to lead me into tomorrow. See what I mean?"

"I think so."

"Let's say I was heading out for two days across the desert, where I knew there was no water—now, if I drank all the water I was carrying the first day, that would have definite results. Do you know what that result would be?"

"You wouldn't have any water left!"

"Right," Hawk laughed. "Everything's like that, though maybe not so easy to see. Tell me, Zack, do you believe God is good or God is evil?"

"How could He be anything but good?"

"All right, then let's say you are caught out in a terrible thunderstorm, and lighting's flashing down nearby—you think you might be scared?"

"Likely so."

"If God is good, why would you be scared? Won't He take care of you?"

"Yeah, I reckon so."

"Who made the lightning and the thunderstorm?"

"God."

"And you say He's good?"

"Yeah."

"If He's good, won't He take care of you?"

"I reckon. But people still get killed in storms, and in lots of other ways too," I said.

"Does that mean God *isn't* good?"

"No, I reckon He still must be."

"Even if people are dying?"

MODULE 3: INTEGRITY   **CHARACTER FORMATION**
SESSION 15: An Honest Thinker   **Grades 1 - 5**

"People have to die."

"And God is still good?"

"Yeah."

"Do you see what I'm aiming at, Zack? If you say God is good, then it must mean something to you. It seems to me that one of the things it means is that you ought not to be afraid. If you say God is good, then you've got to follow out and see where that statement leads you. All the way up the mountains and down the other side . . . clear across the country. There's not much sense believing something if you don't know what the results are going to be."

"Yeah, that seems true enough."

"Lots of folks only follow what they say as far as is convenient for them. Like when they get up high into the mountains or come to a wide river or even the ocean, instead of keeping going to see where their direction leads, they stop their horse, get out of the saddle, and quit. That's why I kept pushing you a while back until you said around the world. You gotta learn to follow your ideas and what you believe all the way to the end like that, too."

"You're always doing that with me, trying to make me look past where I'd get off the horse if I was by myself."

"I try to, Son. It's the only way to be an **HONEST THINKER**. It's the only way to see things like they really are."

"What were you going to say about God being good?" I asked.

"The way I look at it is that saying God is good leads to the conclusion that He's gonna take care of you, no matter what happens. Even if you die, God's still good. Even if you get struck by one of those bolts of lightning, He's still taking care of you, 'cause He's still good. You see—saying you believe something, well, that's got consequences. Thinking it through till the smoke clears, that's what I call it."

"So are you never afraid?" I asked.

"Heck, yes. I'm a man just like every other man. I ain't saying I'm never afraid 'cause sometimes I am. Plenty of times, in fact. I was afraid when I was fighting Demming. A man full of hate fights to kill—they're the hardest to whip, the angry ones. I'm just trying to help you see how you've got to follow ideas out to the end and see what comes of them."

"What about choices?" I said. "You said your choices and what you do leads places and has results too."

"Yeah, and in some ways I reckon the choices a feller makes are even more important than the ideas he holds, 'cause your choices go into making you who you are. That's how your character gets put together—by all the choices you made all your life."

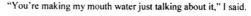

"How do they do that?"

Hawk thought for a minute.

"Let me see if I can say it like this. Imagine your stepma fixing your family a big pot of stew. She might put in some meat and some carrots and potatoes and celery, maybe some onions and peppers, a little salt, maybe some wheat or barley. A stew can have most anything in it, can't it?"

"You're making my mouth water just talking about it," I said.

"Mine too!" said Hawk. "Well, anyway, the fact is that she could make just about any kind of stew she wanted—a beef stew, a chicken stew, a ham stew. It could be thick or thin. It could be mostly vegetables or mostly meat. And what would decide what kind of stew it turned out to be?"

"What she put in the pot?"

"That's it exactly! That's why every stew's likely just a tad different from every other stew."

"And that's just like people, right?"

"Now you're getting it, Zack, my boy! Exactly like people. We're all different, too, depending on what *we* put in our *own* pots."

"You're saying I'm like a stew."

Hawk laughed.

"Did I say that?"

"You *implied* it," I said.

"You got me there! Thinking it through 'til the smoke clears—you're a quick learner!"

"So am I like a stew?"

"I reckon you are. So am I. So is every man or woman alive. We're cooking it up ourselves, all our lives, throwing in new ingredients all the time. The more kindness we throw into the pot, the more kindness there is in the stew.

The more unselfishness we put in, the more unselfish our character will become. But a man like Demming, who's been tossing in anger and bitterness and hatred and selfishness all his life, why, by this time his is a pretty foul-smelling batch of stuff I sure wouldn't want to come near."

MODULE 3: INTEGRITY
SESSION 15: An Honest Thinker

CHARACTER FORMATION
Grades 1 - 5

"But does what you did when you were a kid matter that much?" I asked.

"You bet it does. Everything goes into the pot."

"But half the time you don't know no better."

"It ain't so much that every tiny thing has that big an effect. But every bit of bitterness or anger or selfishness you throw in your stew makes it easier to add more the next time. So what you do when you're young matters a lot if it means you get headed in a certain direction and you keep going that way and never turn your head toward someplace else. The anger and selfishness gets all the more natural the more of it you put in the stew, till before long you're just an angry, selfish person. You just kept putting those kinds of choices into your stew until that's all it tastes like."

Sounds kinda hopeless if you're a brat when you're little."

"Nah, nothing's hopeless. All you gotta do is point your horse in a new direction . . . make a new, better-tasting stew. It's just that most folks don't take the energy to go someplace else than where their horse is already going. Too much work for them."

"But how does somebody make a new kind of stew if it's already full of bad-tasting vittles?"

"It might take a little time, but you just gotta start putting better-tasting things into it. And there ain't no law against sticking a spoon in the pot and taking something out, either. What would your stepma do if she threw a big onion into her stew and then realized it was rotten and was gonna spoil the whole thing? Likely she'd fish it out pronto, right?"

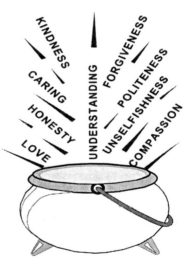

TALK ABOUT IT

(questions to talk about with learners after
the story with possible answers in brackets)

1. **How did Zack and Hawk meet?** [They met when Zack fell into a ravine and broke his legs.
Hawk nursed him back to health.]

2. **What did Hawk mean when he said that every idea and choice leads to something else?**
[Each idea or choice has consequences. Everything has outcomes and repercussions. Every idea
and choice has implications, which Hawk says are like footprints.]

3. **Why was Hawk always looking around, down the trail, up the mountains, ahead and
behind all the time?** [He wanted to keep a few steps ahead of himself in his thoughts and
choices. If he said or did something, he wanted to know what it would lead to.]

4. **Why did Hawk ask Zack if he believed God was good or evil?** [He wanted Zack to see the
results of his belief. He wanted Zack to see where his belief would end if he followed it through
to the end.]

5. **What conclusions did Hawk draw from the belief that God is good?** [If God is good, He is
going to take care of you, no matter what happens. Even if you die, God is still good. He is still
taking care of you.]

6. **How did Hawk say a person's character is put together?** [A person's character is put together
by all the choices you make all your life.]

7. **What image did Hawk use to explain how a character is built?** [He used the image of a stew.]

8. **How does Hawk explain that a person's character is like a stew?** [Just as a stew has many
ingredients, so does a person's character. Just as every stew is different from every other, people
are different too, depending on what they put into their character stew (life). If constructive
thoughts, words, attitudes, and actions are put in, it will be a good stew, a constructive character.
If destructive thoughts, words, attitudes, and actions are added, it will be a destructive stew (life),
a destructive character.]

9. **How do the choices people make when they are young make a difference?** [The choices
people make when they are young head them in a certain direction. Most people keep heading in
the direction they started. Every bit of bitterness, anger, or selfishness that is thrown in the stew
(life) makes it easier to add more the next time. Likewise, every bit of kindness, forgiveness,
truth, or respect makes it easier to head in the direction of constructive choices.]

10. **What can be done if wrong choices have already been made and a person's "stew" (life) is
beginning to taste bad (to be destructive)?** [The person would need to turn in a new direction
and begin to make better stew (choices) . He or she would need to start putting into the stew

MODULE 3: INTEGRITY **CHARACTER FORMATION**
SESSION 15: An Honest Thinker Grades 1 - 5

character virtues that result in constructive choices and stop putting in character traits that result in destructive choices. A person may need to "take out" some of the destructive choices.]

11. **What are some character traits that would result in a destructive character stew (life)?**
[Indifference, revenge, dishonesty, resentfulness, selfishness.]

12. **What are some character virtues that would make a constructive character stew (life)?**
[Kindness, forgiveness, generosity, patience, love. An additional list may be found on Student Activity Page 2.]

ACTIVITIES
to
Apply-Practice-Transform-Transfer
Integrity

Define Two Words

 Preparation/Materials Needed: Copies of Student Activity Page 1, one for each learner; dictionaries; paper and pencils, or a tape/DVD recorder.

 <u>**Guided Conversation:**</u>

On the student activity page I am giving you are two words, *outcome* and *repercussion.*

Look up both words in the dictionary. Then write, or record on tape or DVD, a definition for each word.

After you have completed the definitions, choose and do one of the following:
1. Write a sentence using each of the words.
2. Write a poem using one of the words.
3. Draw a cartoon showing an outcome or repercussion.

[Here are some common definitions:

Outcome: An end; a final consequence; aftermath; consequences; something that follows as a result; an effect of something said or done.

Repercussion: A widespread, indirect, or unforeseen effect of something done or said; result; effect; backlash; impact; consequence.]

MODULE 3: INTEGRITY   **CHARACTER FORMATION**
SESSION 15: An Honest Thinker   **Grades 1 - 5**

Make Your Own Character Stew

Preparation/Materials Needed: Copies of Student Activity Page 2, one for each learner; pencils or felt markers.

Guided Conversation:

In the story, Hawk and Zack talked about a "character stew." Hawk said we are all like stew. He said, "We're cooking it up ourselves, all our lives, throwing in new ingredients all the time. The more kindness we throw into the pot, the more kindness there is in the stew (our life). The more unselfishness we put in, the more unselfish our character will become. You just gotta start putting better-tasting things into it."

On Student Activity Page 2 is a list of character virtues that might make a tasty "character stew." Circle the character traits that you can honestly say are a part of your character right now.

On the stew pot, print the character words you circled to begin to make your character stew. When you have completed printing the words on the pot, consider what other ingredients (character virtues) you would like to add. Be an "honest thinker."

Perhaps you could ask someone to help you think honestly about the character virtues you need added to your life. List these virtues along the sides of the pot.

STUDENT ACTIVITY PAGE 2,
MAKE YOUR OWN CHARACTER STEW

Compassion	Joy	Wisdom	Courage
Love	Peace	Respect	Generosity
Kindness	Thankfulness	Tolerance	Boldness
Self-Esteem	Gratitude	Courtesy	Cooperation
Obedience	Integrity	Responsibility	Authority
Gentleness	Truth	Discipline	Goodness
Empathy	Honesty	Self-Control	Humor
Forgiveness	Discernment	Dependability	Perseverance
Humility	Faithfulness	Initiative	Endurance
Diligence	Loyalty		

Print the character words you circles on the stew pot to begin to make your character stew. Write your name on the tag on the handle.

INDEX

Corrections:

pg 14

pg. 19 (go to A for readiness ideas. But only 1 there!)
   Oh— also grids for Integrity!

pg. 81   your = you're
pg-118- chg. words?

Made in the USA